# Eyewitness
# DANCE

Tibetan
dance mask

Bharata
natyam
dancer

Ballet tutu

Nigerian
dance staff

Headdress for
ballet dancer

Javanese ear
and arm
ornaments

Dancing
bodhisattva

Costume
designs

Pointe ballet shoes

Jewelry for bharata natyam

# Eyewitness
# DANCE

Written by
DR. ANDRÉE GRAU

The fish dive, popular in classical ballet

DK Publishing, Inc.

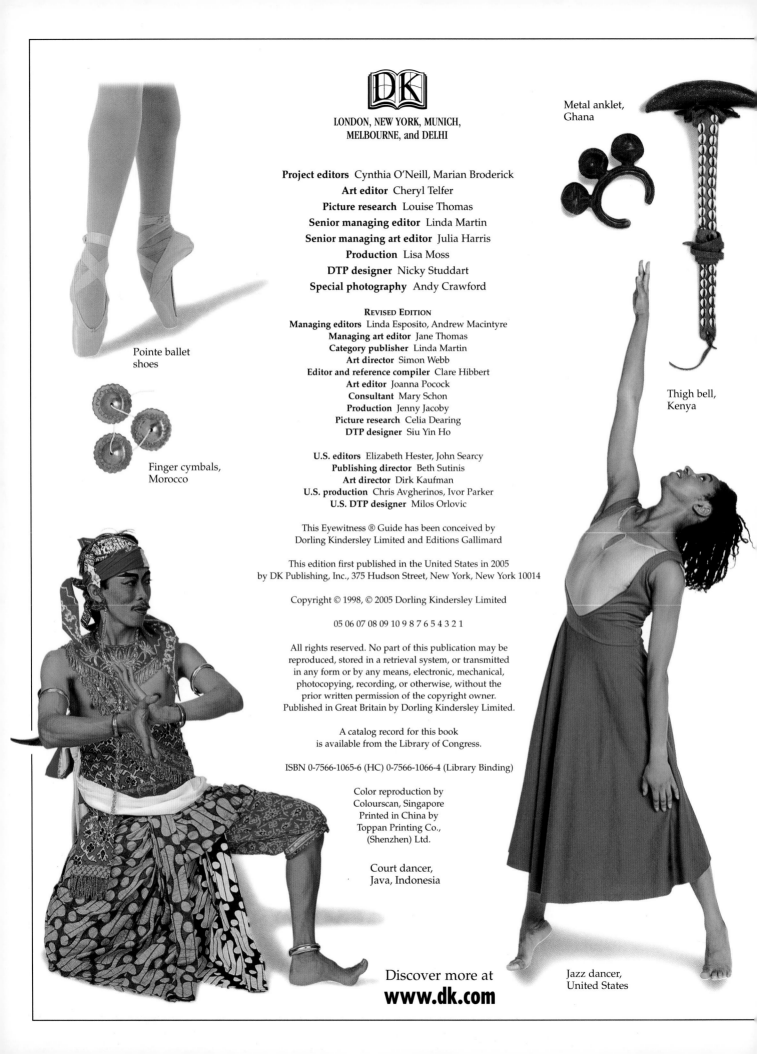

**DK**

LONDON, NEW YORK, MUNICH,
MELBOURNE, and DELHI

Metal anklet,
Ghana

**Project editors** Cynthia O'Neill, Marian Broderick
**Art editor** Cheryl Telfer
**Picture research** Louise Thomas
**Senior managing editor** Linda Martin
**Senior managing art editor** Julia Harris
**Production** Lisa Moss
**DTP designer** Nicky Studdart
**Special photography** Andy Crawford

REVISED EDITION
**Managing editors** Linda Esposito, Andrew Macintyre
**Managing art editor** Jane Thomas
**Category publisher** Linda Martin
**Art director** Simon Webb
**Editor and reference compiler** Clare Hibbert
**Art editor** Joanna Pocock
**Consultant** Mary Schon
**Production** Jenny Jacoby
**Picture research** Celia Dearing
**DTP designer** Siu Yin Ho

**U.S. editors** Elizabeth Hester, John Searcy
**Publishing director** Beth Sutinis
**Art director** Dirk Kaufman
**U.S. production** Chris Avgherinos, Ivor Parker
**U.S. DTP designer** Milos Orlovic

Pointe ballet
shoes

Finger cymbals,
Morocco

Thigh bell,
Kenya

This Eyewitness ® Guide has been conceived by
Dorling Kindersley Limited and Editions Gallimard

This edition first published in the United States in 2005
by DK Publishing, Inc., 375 Hudson Street, New York, New York 10014

A catalog record for this book
is available from the Library of Congress.

ISBN 0-7566-1065-6 (HC) 0-7566-1066-4 (Library Binding)

Color reproduction by
Colourscan, Singapore
Printed in China by
Toppan Printing Co.,
(Shenzhen) Ltd.

Court dancer,
Java, Indonesia

Discover more at
**www.dk.com**

Jazz dancer,
United States

# Contents

Kathkali
dancer, India

# What is dance?

DANCE IS A SERIES OF MOVEMENTS performed in patterns and set to an accompaniment. Every human society practices dance, which may be performed solo, in couples, or in groups. People around the world use dance to express themselves, pass on their histories, and exercise their bodies. In this way, dance can be a celebration of the emotional, mental, and physical human self. It can also be a preparation for battle or an unspoken protest. Dance is often used to mark major life changes or to commemorate an important event in a nation's history. In the earliest societies, dance helped humans survive – it was a way for communities to learn cooperation in working and hunting together – and, like today, dance was probably used to communicate and express feelings that are difficult to convey in any other way.

Dinka folk dancer, Sudan, Africa

*Steps of difficult folk dances take time to master*

**JOY OF DANCE**
When experiencing great joy, we often feel an urge to leap and dance. For many people, Gene Kelly's exuberant dancing in the film *Singin' in the Rain* (1952) is a perfect illustration of the joy of dance.

**LOST DANCES**
Dances, unlike many other works of art, are not fixed in time – they exist only while being performed. Many dances, such as the galliard of the 16th century, are no longer performed, and the moves are now lost. An early engraving gives us only the faintest idea of what the galliard might have looked like.

**DANCES AS A FOLK FORM**
Certain dances are created by and belong to particular groups of people and are passed down through generations. In many parts of Africa, these dances can reinforce a people's sense of identity, or can be used to celebrate rituals or rites of passage.

**DANCE AS AN ART FORM**
Modern dance has generally been against the classical forms, such as ballet. However, some contemporary dancers have retained the visual poetry of classical dance – both European and African – while mixing it with impulsive gestures from folk and street dance, creating a new art form.

*Briefly held statuelike poses come from the classical tradition*

*Classical leg shapes of ballet*

*Modern hand movements*

*An "isolation," in which one body part moves independently of the others*

*A graceful improvisation from folk or street dances*

*Eye contact adds to the sensuality of the tango*

*Body shapes are perfectly symmetrical*

*Clothing is chosen to emphasize the swirling fluidity of jazz dance movements*

*Foot moves echo those of ballet*

*Barefoot dancing is one way of throwing off the traditions of the past*

## BANNED DANCES

Some dances are disapproved of so much by society that they are banned. In 1913, German army and navy personnel could be dismissed for dancing the tango. In 1956, during one of Elvis Presley's first television appearances, cameras showed him only from the waist up, because the gyrating movements of his hips were considered shocking.

## ORDER AND RHYTHM

In ancient Greece, dance was seen as the gift of the immortals. The Greek word, *chora,* meaning "source of joy," resembles *choros,* the Greek word for "dance." Order and rhythm, the main qualities of dance, were also the qualities of the gods. The philosopher Plato wrote that dance "gave the body its just proportions."

Buddhist dancing figure, China

## SACRED DANCES

Many religions, such as Buddhism and Hinduism, use dance as a part of worship, and dancing figures are often seen in shrines of these faiths. Other religions have ritual gestures instead of dance – special movements performed by priests while reading from sacred texts, or special postures adopted while praying. In medieval times, walking the maze of Chartres Cathedral in France was part of religious worship.

# Learning to dance

WE ALL LEARN to dance in our own way, whether by imitation or instruction. Different societies have different ideals for a dancer's body. Some dancers, including Southeast Asian classical dancers, are expected to have a particular look. Every day they practice exercises that develop their muscles and posture in specific ways, creating extraordinary dancers' bodies. Other dance styles accept a variety of body shapes and sizes, but all require great stamina and flexibility. In some places, dances are only for young people, and performers retire when they reach middle age, or even before. Other societies appreciate that dancers acquire more depth in their style as they grow older.

*For practice, Cambodian dancers wear comfortable clothes, but they are literally sewn into their costumes for performances*

*Thumb and index finger create a classic offering gesture*

**CLASSICAL CAMBODIAN DANCE**
A slow, almost hypnotic pace, and smooth wavelike movements characterize the classical dance of Cambodia. To achieve the effect, dancers need to develop a high degree of articulation, or flexibility, in all their joints. Students practice special exercises that make their fingers and elbows so supple that they appear to be without bones.

*A walking step*

*Flexibility of the ankle joint is important, as it helps dancers move in a gliding fashion*

*A cyclic pattern that twists and spirals, from the center of the body*

**MARTHA GRAHAM**
For Martha Graham (1894–1991), there was nothing more wonderful than the human body. She saw dance as a celebration of the miracle of the body's beauty, and she called dancers "athletes of God." Like athletes, her dancers were expected to move in a disciplined way and to carry out a daily regime of exercises based on her principles of contraction, release, and spiral. Graham's dances were designed to reveal a person's inner landscape – what she called the "cave of the heart."

*The Song, choreographed by Martha Graham, 1985*

**DOING THE SAMBA, BRAZIL**
The samba is a fast-moving dance that, like many South American dances, has African and Caribbean roots. In preparation for Rio de Janeiro's annual carnival, dancers practice for months in samba schools – neighborhood social clubs whose main purpose is to organize carnival processions. A prize is awarded every year to the best samba school, and competition is fierce.

*Graham's dances incorporated a lot of floor work*

### LEARNING TO DANCE IN BALI

In Bali, Indonesia, dance lessons tend to be public occasions where everyone is free to watch. The Balinese are interested not only in dance performance but in the entire learning process. Children learn dance forms mainly through imitation (known as nuwutin), but dance teachers also manipulate the limbs of their young students by placing them in the correct positions. Even before a child begins formal instruction – maybe even before he or she can walk – relatives bend the child's arms and hands into the correct positions.

*Stylized and graceful dance, such as that of Japan, suits older dancers*

*Symmetry is usually an important part of Japanese dance*

*Balinese children learn to achieve a tranquil, masklike facial expression*

*A quiet intensity and alert eyes characterize most Balinese dance*

*The gracefulness of arm and hand movements are a major part of Balinese dance*

*Arms are held at sharp angles*

### OLD AND YOUNG

Dance is not the prerogative of the young – in Asia, for example, older dancers are admired. Both youthful and elderly Japanese celebrate the coming of spring once a year by dancing at sakura festivals. With the cherry blossom trees spectacularly full of bloom, the dancers honor the beauty and short lifespan of their national flower.

*Torso is held straight with a slightly arched spine and the shoulders slightly up*

*Brightly colored material is made into a sarong and wrapped around the dancer*

*Limbo pole is lowered after each successful attempt, to add a competitive element*

*Fire makes the dance even more of a display – and even more competitive*

### LIMBO DANCING

Many folk dances have a competitive element. During carnivals and other celebrations in the Caribbean, young dancers often show off and compete with each other by performing dances that include acrobatic feats. One of these, known as the limbo dance, originated in West Africa. While it looks spontaneous, it actually requires a suppleness and agility that is built up over an extended period.

*Balinese dance is performed barefoot*

11

# Ballet class

Each variety of dance is supported by a technique that needs to be mastered by dancers. These techniques have been refined, sometimes over hundreds of years, to create an ideal of beauty. To achieve this ideal, some dancers dedicate their lives to dance, learning their skills through discipline and years of training, starting in childhood. For example, in classical ballet, dancers have to be elegant, long-limbed, and flexible. Although they need amazing stamina, every movement must appear effortless. Ballet dancers, no matter how exalted their position in the company, attend daily classes to keep their bodies in peak condition and to maintain control over their muscles and movements.

**BUILDING STRENGTH**
To make difficult lifts look effortless, male dancers must be strong. Along with studying the steps, boys train using special exercises that build their strength without making their physiques too bulky. These exercises are strictly supervised.

*Exercises to strengthen the upper body are important for male dancers*

**SCHOOLS AND COMPANIES**
Prestigious ballet companies are often affiliated with ballet schools. Many dancers with the world-famous Kirov Ballet (above) began at the Kirov School in St. Petersburg, Russia.

Dance pupils at the Royal Ballet School in London

*Dancers learn basic moves correctly at the barre*

*Back is straight*

*Knees bent over toes*

*Thighs horizontal to floor*

**1 BEGINNER'S EXERCISES**
Among the first movements a beginner learns are pliés (bends) and relevés (rises). These "easy" moves must be practiced many times to get them right. This is the starting position for a grand plié in second.

**2** Pliés help to stretch and strengthen a dancer's leg muscles. The dancer bends smoothly and slowly into a demi-plié (half bend), with his feet turned out and his heels on the floor.

**3** The dancer bends further, into a grand plié (full bend), keeping his heels on the floor. He takes care to keep his movements controlled and smooth throughout.

## LEARNING ARABESQUES

As dance pupils progress, they move on to more difficult movements, such as the arabesque. In this beautiful position, a dancer balances on one leg with her other leg extended behind her and makes a long, slanted line with her body. Dancers are taught the basic kinds of arabesque first, such as the low arabesque, shown at right.

*The upper back is kept straight*

*Head is kept up*

*Front hand is turned palm down, following the line of the arm*

*A diagonal line is created by the left leg and the right arm*

## DEGAS AND THE BALLET

More than half the paintings by the French Impressionist painter Edgar Degas (1834–1917) feature young ballerinas. In his richly colored work, the artist captured behind-the-scenes moments, such as this ballet class. The elderly teacher, leaning on his stick is, in fact, the choreographer Jules Perrot (1810–1894), who earlier in his career choreographed the romantic ballet *Giselle.*

## LIFTING HIGHER

As a dancer builds up strength, she is able to lift her leg higher behind her. Her body makes a beautifully curved line from her raised foot to her shoulder, and she is perfectly balanced. Her arms stretch out softly in flowing harmony with her body.

*Working leg*

*Soft, flowing line*

## ADVANCED ARABESQUES

A pupil who has studied ballet for years can perform more advanced movements such as the move shown at right. The dancer balances on demi-pointe. She turns her head to look over her front shoulder. In this expressive movement, the dancer can raise and lower her working leg in a sweeping motion.

*In a demi-pointe, the dancer stands on the ball of her foot*

*Legs appear to be crossed to the audience*

*Dancers hold the barre for support during certain exercises at the beginning of the class*

## BALLET STUDIOS

Mirrors line the walls of dance studios so that pupils can check their positions during class. The wooden floor is especially constructed to "give" slightly when dancers land from a jump. This protects their joints from uncomfortable jarring. A wooden handrail, known as a barre, runs around the wall.

## ARABESQUE CROISÉ À TERRE

There is a great variety of arabesques, and ballet pupils learn how each can express different moods and feelings. In the arabesque known as croisé à terre, the dancer's back and neck make a graceful line. The dancer concentrates on maintaining the correct placing of her legs and holding her hips level.

13

# Accompaniment

D̲ance usually combines movements with music – but not always. Sometimes dance can be accompanied by other, nonmusical sounds, such as street noise, insect or animal sounds, or even the rhythmic banging of a door. Dance can also be accompanied by meaningful texts, such as beautiful or sacred poetry. It can even be performed in silence. The relationship between dance and its accompaniment varies widely, but musical or otherwise, accompaniment is vital to establishing the right atmosphere. In European and American dance theater, for example, the orchestra is usually hidden from the audience, whereas in other parts of the world, the musicians are often on display and greatly contribute to the visual spectacle.

*Drumsticks can be hit together to create another percussion sound*

**TONGA DANCE**
Traditional sung poetry, often based on myths and legends, accompanies some dances on the Pacific island of Tonga. The dancer interprets important words in the poem. For example, if the text mentions a flower, the dance may represent a breeze carrying the flower's fragrance. The dances are usually performed standing or sitting, and include graceful hand and arm movements.

**CLAPPING AND THE CUECA**
In the cueca, a Chilean dance for couples, guitars provide the main accompaniment, but singers and dancers punctuate the music with handclaps. This lively dance and accompaniment inspired the song "America" in Leonard Bernstein's hit musical *West Side Story*.

**DRUMMING IN AFRICA**
Because Africa is a large continent with more than 50 countries, there is an immense variety of dance music, ranging from unaccompanied traditional singing to the "talking" drums of West Africa, which imitate the sounds of speech. Drum music is also especially popular in Burundi and other parts of East Africa. The drums used in large ensembles, such as the one below, have to be tuned carefully because the melody is as important as the rhythm they provide.

*Drum ensembles usually have a leader*

*Drums are tuned by tightening the wooden screws*

*Animal hide stretched over tree trunk*

Seedpod rattle, Zimbabwe

*Seedpod*

*Cowrie shells*

*Pellet bells*

*Hide*

Copper rings with bells, India

**DANCING FEET**
Body attachments, such as leg rattles, anklets, armbands, or thigh bells, can add a whole new dimension to a dance performance. Though they are not actually "played," an experienced dancer can control them so they accompany the performance. These ornaments are often made from natural materials, such as seedpods, but they can also be made from synthetic materials.

*String*

*Bell*

Metal anklet, Ashanti people, Ghana

Thigh bell, Nandi people, Kenya

Finger cymbals, Berber people, Morocco

**FINGER INSTRUMENTS**
In many parts of the world, dancers carry small instruments that can be played with just the fingers. They range from rings with small bells attached to different types of castanets to cymbals.

**AFRICAN DANCE TRADITIONS**
In many African societies, there are special flat clearings where people can drum and dance. The drumming may be accompanied by singing, clapping, or body slapping – or, as pictured here, by fantastically high leaps and somersaults.

*Split bamboo*

Bamboo rattle, or pu'ili, Hawaii

*Smaller drums produce higher pitches, while larger drums produce lower pitches*

Ninga drummers, Burundi

# Keeping time

W<small>E ALL HAVE A SENSE</small> of ourselves and of other people moving through space and time. In dancers, this sense is highly developed. Dancers are aware of their bodies and of the effect of their movements on an audience. When they are carrying out one action, they are mentally anticipating the next; they subtly adjust the movements leading to the next step, in order to prepare the audience. Performers use rhythm to establish this kind of exchange with an audience. Rhythm is a timing system that develops on a basic pattern of silences and pauses. Performers cannot ignore the laws of rhythm, and cannot dance without a sense of rhythm, but they can carve out their own ways of interpreting it. Whether it is the fast, exciting rhythms of the Spanish flamenco, or the slow, controlled rhythms of Japanese nō, successful dancers create their own timing on top of a basic rhythmic pattern.

**TIWI PEOPLE, AUSTRALIA**
Among the Tiwi Aboriginal people of Melville and Bathurst islands, clear lines and rhythm are essential for movements to be considered dance. These performers specialize in "strong dancing," where every change must occur exactly on the beat. Movements flowing across the rhythm exist in the Tiwi repertoire, but they are performed only as song gestures.

*Sumptuous costumes are made of gold and silver brocade*

*Masks used in nō are an art form in themselves*

*Nō relies on symbolism, often provided by props*

**NOH DANCERS**
The Japanese dance-drama noh is a majestic and beautiful art form. The gestures, breathing, and music in each scene of each performance are underlined by the complex idea of *Jo-ha-kyu*, which concerns the rhythmic relationship between two forces pulling in opposite directions. Noh is very slow-moving, and performances are extremely long. It has been compared to watching a flower change imperceptibly and eventually shed its petals.

*Kathak dancers occasionally dance in pairs*

**KATHAK**
In Indian music, rhythm is expressed by tal, a system of beats that gives a dance its structure. The dancers of kathak, an energetic dance form from northern India, are expert at improvising intricate steps with their feet while making graceful movements with their arms. Kathak dancers are involved in a "conversation" with musicians, which develops as the performance goes on. They explore the cycle of beats individually, but at key moments of the music cycle they synchronize their timing.

## FOUR TEMPERAMENTS

Listening to some music, George Balanchine (1904–1983) was moved "to try to make visible not only the rhythm, melody, and harmony but even the timbres [tones] of the instruments." In 1946, he set a ballet to Paul Hindemith's *The Four Temperaments* that tried to represent, through pure dance, what was in the composer's mind musically.

*The Four Temperaments, 1946*

*A scene from Choreartium (1933)*

## FLAMENCO

The origins of the flamboyant Spanish dance known as flamenco are obscure. Some say flamenco originated in the southern province of Andalusia. Others say it came to Andalusia with gypsies, who traveled from India and Pakistan via Egypt and that the roots of flamenco are in the kathak. In both flamenco and kathak, sophisticated footwork creates rhythmic patterns and the dance itself acts as percussion. Improvisation may still be practiced, and dialogue with the musicians is crucial in both.

*Elegant arm and hand movements of flamenco are sometimes reinforced with the use of a fan*

*Performers manipulate their costumes as part of the dance*

## SYMPHONIC BALLET

In the 1930s, the Russian choreographer Léonide Massine created a number of ballets set to symphonies. *Choreartium,* which was set to Brahms' Fourth Symphony, was his second. Although other choreographers had previously arranged ballets to symphonies, they were isolated productions. Debate raged around Massine's work – some people felt that dancing to symphonic music somehow debased the symphony.

*Castanets are not a traditional part of flamenco but are used in the folk dances of southern Spain*

*Musicians sometimes hit the wood of the guitar to add another percussive sound*

## FLAMENCO AND ACCOMPANIMENT

The three main components in flamenco are singing (cante), dancing (baile), and guitar (guitarra). Performances originally included only singing and dancing, with some handclapping (toque de palmas). The guitar came later, first as accompaniment, then as a solo instrument in its own right.

*Special shoes have nails driven into the soles and heels are used to add percussion*

# Themes and messages

Dance does not always simply tell a story. It may be used to bring people together, by reinforcing their shared beliefs about their place in the world or celebrating their relationship with the supernatural. Some dances, such as the Native American ghost dance, were created to channel frustration and bring hope for the future. Others, such as the haka of New Zealand, are war dances that can raise aggression against enemies. Some communal African dances teach the young the values of society by showing the path they are expected to follow. In contrast, other dances, such as modern antiwar ballets, challenge society's values and inspire new ideas.

*Club represents the owner's supernatural helper*

Arapaho ghost dance club, 1800s

### GHOST DANCE
This dance was a response by the Native Americans of the Great Plains to intolerable poverty and oppression. Carrying carved clubs, they danced in appeal to their gods to restore traditional ways and bring back the buffalo. The dance was banned by the white authorities.

### DANCING AGAINST WAR
With his ballet *The Green Table* (1932), Kurt Jooss tried to move people to take action against the evil political system of fascism, which was overtaking Europe in the 1930s. The ballet is about the two-faced nature of some diplomats, and how they must shoulder the responsibility for the deaths caused by war.

Kurt Jooss

### BUFFALO DANCE
The buffalo dance, as shown in this 19th-century painting, carries a message of respect for the animals that are about to be killed. Tribes such as the Blackfoot promised the buffalo that life taken from it in this world would be returned in the next. They believed that a sacred ritual dance had the power to make this happen

*Buffalo heads worn during the dance*

*Dancers entered a hypnotic state*

*Masks worn by the dancers*

*Shouting and warlike gestures accompany the haka*

*Traditional wooden weapons are used as part of the haka*

### DANCING FOR WAR
Throughout the world, dance has been used to drill warriors, both to strengthen their muscles in preparation for hand-to-hand combat and to unify the fighters. The Maori people of New Zealand traditionally performed a war dance known as the haka before battle and in victory celebrations afterward. Today, New Zealand rugby teams prepare for their matches in world competitions by performing the haka before kickoff.

**GREAT DOMBA SONG**
Among the Venda of South Africa, young women prepare for marriage and integration into adult life by learning the milayos – the laws set out in poems and riddles – and dancing the domba. The domba requires extremely good timing and cooperation.

**HARVESTS AND CROPS**
Dances are performed at harvest festivals around the world to celebrate the end of a successful farming year. The ritual is thought to help regenerate the earth in preparation for the next harvest. Such dances also promote social unity and cooperation in the face of the dangers and whims of nature.

*Ankle or shin bells add to the rhythm of the dance*

*The colors blue and yellow represent a town called Letchworth in the heart of England*

*Fresh flowers adorn hats to represent spring and regeneration*

**MORRIS COSTUME**
Morris dancers emphasize group unity by dressing alike. They wear white shirts, flowered straw hats, and ornamental sashes known as baldrics. Morris costume sometimes includes bells attached to the shin that ring in time with the movements of the dance.

**MORRIS DANCE**
Traditionally performed at local festivals in the South Midlands of England, morris dancing is performed today throughout the country. It was once an exclusively male ceremonial dance but now is danced by amateurs of both sexes – often in competitions. Categories of the dances include processional, jig, and set dancing. Team dancing is deliberately boisterous – this reinforces team spirit amongthe participants, especially in competition.

*Sticks or handkerchiefs are often used*

*Baldrics*

*Team colors*

# Telling tales

*Firebird is dressed in red*

*This move is designed to indicate struggle – the prince is forcing the firebird to help him*

DANCE TELLS STORIES in many ways. Some dances use mime, facial expressions, and movements that have specific meanings. For example, kathakali performers in southern India use a code of gesture that literally translates the text sung by an accompanying vocalist. Often, however, dance uses stories that are already well-known. Western audiences know the story of *Sleeping Beauty* from childhood, while Indian children are taught the many mischievous adventures of the god Krishna, his ways with milkmaids, and his love for the beautiful Rhada. In every society, people watch dance because it has the power to bring a special interpretation to these popular tales. The very deepest human emotions – love, betrayal, despair – can all be expressed in dance.

**BURMESE PUPPET**
In the puppet theaters of Southeast Asia, well-known stories are told by Burmese marionettes, like the one above, Indonesian shadow puppets, and Vietnamese water puppets.

**FIGHT BETWEEN GOOD AND EVIL**
Ballet stories are often about love winning against cruelty and malice. In *The Firebird* (1910), a magical bird of fire helps Prince Ivan rescue a beautiful princess and rid the world of an evil magician known as Kostchei.

*Prince Albrecht wooing Giselle*

*Giselle plucking a daisy*

*Iconic gesture of flute playing always represents the god Krishna*

*Lion face*

*Fish*

**BHARATA NATYA**
The classical Indian dance form bharata natya blends two very different but complementary types of movements: expressive dance, which interprets classical poetry through mime, and abstract dance with rhythmic improvisation. Hand gestures and stylized facial expressions (abhinaya) are crucial.

**ELOQUENT HANDS**
Hand gestures in bharata natya are known as hasta or mudras. Some hand gestures are iconic – they look like what they represent. Others are symbolic – they are abstract gestures.

**STORY OF GISELLE**
The ballet *Giselle* (1841) tells of a simple village girl overwhelmed by the attention of Albrecht, a prince disguised as a peasant. When Giselle discovers that Albrecht has deceived her and is already engaged, she goes mad and dies of a broken heart. She joins the Wilis, the spirits of young girls betrayed in love. In Act I, Giselle's symbolic movements, such as playing he-loves-me-he-loves-me-not with a flower, emphasize her innocence.

**EXPRESSING EMOTION THROUGH DANCE**
A pas de deux in ballet is a dance for two performers, usually a man and a woman. It presents a relationship – often a beautiful vision of romantic love – from its first awakening to the great joy of its realization. The dancing of a pas de deux can be intimate, or extravagant and full of passion. Between sections of dancing together, each performer traditionally performs a solo dance, known as a variation, showing his and her individuality.

*This arabesque penché (bent forward) is one of the most beautiful expressions of romantic love*

*Disgust*

*Valor*

*Ornate, romantic costumes create the right mood for a love story*

*Male dancers always look at the ballerina*

**KATHAKALI**
Performers of this Indian dance develop phenomenal control over their facial muscles, eyes, and lower and upper eyelids. Through stylized facial expressions, a huge range of emotions, such as valor, revulsion, love, anger, compassion, derision, wonder, and fear can be conveyed to the audience.

*Dancers train from childhood to achieve great strength yet softness in the hands*

*Serene expression is part of the choreography*

*Strong knees and thighs are essential for supporting and lifting*

**CELESTIAL NYMPH**
Thai dancers, like Indian dancers, tell of the heroic mythological beings from the *Ramayana*, an ancient epic poem. However, unlike the Indian hasta, Thai hand gestures do not tell the story literally, but are designed to add beauty and grace to the overall shape of a dance.

*Fingers, palms, and wrists contribute to the overall shape of the dance*

21

# Beauty and strength

PEOPLE EVERYWHERE TAKE PLEASURE in beautiful objects, music, and dance. Yet what is seen as graceful or lovely in one culture can be thought ugly or inappropriate in another. For example, it is shocking for a traditional Indonesian audience to see a ballerina extend her legs, because in Indonesian dance women do not display their legs in this way. Around the world, there are many different sets of rules that decide "good" and "bad" taste. All the members of a community share these rules – but occasionally artists bend or disregard them to introduce new ideas and overcome boundaries.

**JAVANESE COURT DANCER, INDONESIA**
At the sultan's court on the Indonesian island of Java, there is a pure dance style called bedoya, which is performed only by women. The Javanese court dancer must seem to move smoothly and effortlessly. Her graceful, rolling movements are thought to represent the spiritual refinement and wisdom of kingship.

*Gilt-edged sampur*

*Gentle angles or slow movements convey the serenity and elegance of the dance*

**ROYAL RWANDANS**
The royal Tutsi dancers of Rwanda reenact past heroic deeds. This dance commemorates the courageous defense of the kingdom from cattle raiders. The dancers try to represent the vigor and nobility of an ideal warrior. The dancers are accompanied by the royal drums, and symbolize the king's authority.

*Legs are kept hidden in Indonesian dance*

*Hair ornament*

*Ear ornament*

**ADORNMENTS**
Javanese dancers wear delicate jewelry and accessories, such as ear ornaments made from gilded buffalo hide. Their dancing also contains stylized gestures such as playing with earrings or adjusting a head ornament.

*Armlet*

**FLOWING WATER**
Female classical dancers on Java embody the Javanese ideals of beauty, proper behavior, and spiritual growth. In both dance and life, Javanese custom has it that a woman's movements should be quiet, restrained, and modest – and as calming as flowing water. This dancer gently waves her sampur, or scarf, to emphasize the grace and flow of her movements.

*Feet are kept close together and stay in contact with the floor*

*The higher the leap, the more prestige the Cossack dancer gains*

**MALE DANCER, JAVA, INDONESIA**
Unlike female dancers, whose feet scarcely lose contact with the floor, Javanese male dancers – usually depicting warriors – execute wide, sweeping movements and postures. Similarly, while the focus for a female dancer's eyes is generally limited to the floor for a distance of two to five steps, the forceful male dancer can extend the focus of his eyes forward to a distance three times his height.

*The design of these gilded ear ornaments is of Hindu origin*

**COSSACK LEAPS**
In many cultures, only men perform high jumps. Russian soldiers known as Cossacks, for example, use their vital dance style to show off their agility, physical prowess, and technical skills. The Cossacks like to compete for prestige by outdoing each other's acrobatic feats.

*The heroes of one popular dance-drama, the Ramayana, are usually portrayed as archers*

*This angular Javanese stance is based on an ancient Indian posture*

*Leg lifted so that thigh is parallel with the floor*

*Heroic dance often features traditional weapons, such as a sword, as part of the costume*

*Brown is one of the most popular colors used in Javanese costume*

**HIGHLAND LEAPS**
While some dance forms are "earthed," almost caressing the ground, others use high leaps that seem to defy gravity. Scottish Highland dance emphasizes both elevation and swift foot movements, which contrast sharply with the stiffness of the upper body.

*Hands are together in a gesture of reverence*

*Sharp angles created by arms*

**CREATING A WARRIOR**
This Javanese dancer achieves a regal and martial posture by straightening his body, forcing his wrists and elbows into sharp angles, and creating another wide angle with his knee. In contrast to Western ballet's extended foot, Javanese dancers tense the toes upward.

*Wide leg gestures are acceptable for male dancers*

*Weight-bearing leg is kept straight*

*Foot and knee must be turned out sideways*

# Fancy footwear

MOST DANCE STYLES are about the way dancers use their feet. Whether shaped by special shoes or left free, dancers' feet determine their basic postures and movements of a dance. The development of ballet shoes shows how footwear and dance styles influence each other. Until the 1810s, ballerinas wore simple slippers and kept the balls of theirfeet in contact with the floor. However, audiences wanted ballerinas to seem as light as air, and this led to dancing en pointe (on the tip of the toes). To dance this way, ballerinas relied on specially constructed reinforced shoes.

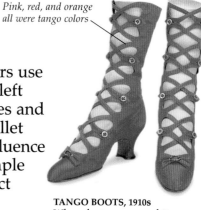

*Pink, red, and orange all were tango colors*

**TANGO BOOTS, 1910s**
When the tango craze hit Europe in the early 20th century, dancers opted for boots in hot "tango colors."

**TIPPYTOES**
Since its invention in the 1810s, dancing en pointe has been identified with classical ballet techniques.

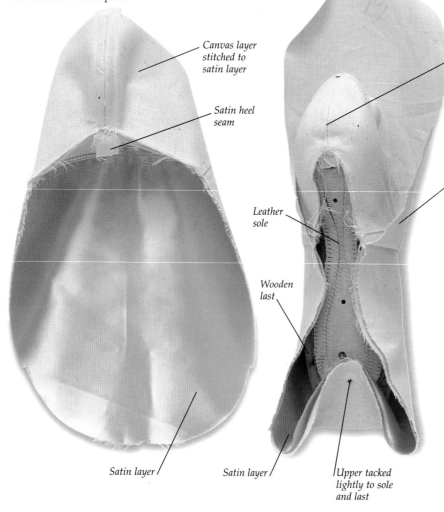

Canvas layer stitched to satin layer

Satin heel seam

Satin layer

Heel seam

One layer of canvas pulled back

Leather sole

Wooden last

Satin layer

Upper tacked lightly to sole and last

**3** The shoemaker pastes layers of card, paper, and burlap around the toe of the shoe, using a flour-and-water glue. The drying process takes two to three hours, forming a block that will support the dancer's toes.

Burlap and paper folded around toe of shoe

Card

White paper

Burlap

Different thicknesses of gray paper

**1 MAKING A BALLET SHOE**
In performance, female ballet dancers generally wear pointe shoes. These are so called because of the hardened block of burlap and paper that allows the dancer to dance en pointe. Despite the delicate appearance of the satin upper, these shoes are quite stiff. The shoemaker begins the shoe by stitching together satin and canvas layers to make the upper.

**2** After turning the upper inside out, the shoemaker tacks a leather sole onto a wooden last (a model of a foot). He then pulls the inside-out upper onto the last and peels back one layer of canvas. The shoemaker tacks the upper to the last, through the leather sole.

*Ankle bells accompany the dancer as she stamps her feet*

*Designs painted on with henna emphasize the curved lines of the feet*

### PAINTED FEET
In bharata natya, a classical Indian dance style, performers decorate their feet instead of wearing shoes. The designs complement the patterns painted on their hands.

*Platform soles decorated with rhinestones*

### PLATFORM SOLES
Performers in traditional dance forms such as Japanese kabuki and Chinese opera wear shoes with elevated soles. Platforms have also been popular in more informal contexts, such as the disco fashions of the 1970s.

### STILT DANCERS
In areas of southern and western Africa, dancers perform on stilts up to six feet (two meters) high. Leg-crossing, jumps, and twirls are precarious, but that is partly the point of the stilt dance. Finding the right balance symbolizes the wisdom of humankind.

*Stilt dancer, Ivory Coast*

*Heel*

*Shoe turned right side out*

*Sole is stitched to upper*

*Layer of canvas is pulled forward to cover the paper-and-glue block*

*Wax thread*

*Canvas is stitched in tight pleats around the block*

*Shoemaker's mark*

*Leather insole*

*Drawstring*

*Dancers soften new shoes to shape them to their feet – some soften shoes by closing them in a door!*

*Satin ribbons, normally about 1 in (2.5 cm) wide and 1.5 ft (50 cm) long*

**4** When the glue has dried, the peeled-back layer of canvas is pulled forward and pleated around the toe with metal pincers. The shoemaker stitches the hard leather sole to the upper, using wax thread. The shoe is removed from the last and turned the right way out. A leather insole is then inserted before the shoe is put back on the last.

**5** The shoemaker shapes and fashions the shoe with a special smooth hammer. This tool is also used to shape the pointe into a platform. Finally, the finished shoes are put into a warm oven to harden for 12 to 15 hours.

**6** Traditionally, dancers sew the ribbons onto their own shoes and often embroider the toe area to stop the fabric from fraying. Pointe shoes have a remarkably short life; principal dancers in a ballet company wear out about a dozen pairs a month!

# Makeup

*Traditional makeup is applied with an erkila, a stick made from a stripped coconut leaf*

Throughout the world, performers apply makeup to dramatize their features. Whether they use ochers, charcoal, synthetic materials, or paints made from powdered stones, makeup has many uses. It highlights beauty; transforms humans into heroes, demons, or animals; or acts as a mask, hiding a dancer's identity. In India, kathakali performers use makeup to transform themselves into mythical beings. In Africa, Woodabe men use makeup and dance to express their inner beauty.

**1 APPLYING KATHAKALI MAKEUP**
In kathakali, a dance-drama from South India, an artist applies layers of makeup. The colorful and elaborate designs, which take up to four hours to complete, have been handed down over centuries.

**"STILL LIFE" AT THE PENGUIN CAFÉ**
The stunning costumes and makeup used in the modern ballet *"Still Life" at the Penguin Café* helped to reinforce its ecological message about endangered species.

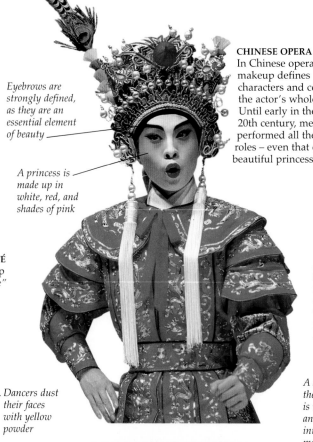

*Eyebrows are strongly defined, as they are an essential element of beauty*

**CHINESE OPERA**
In Chinese opera, makeup defines characters and covers the actor's whole face. Until early in the 20th century, men performed all the roles – even that of beautiful princesses!

*A princess is made up in white, red, and shades of pink*

*The chutti alters the shape of the actor's face*

**2 ATTACHING THE CHUTTI**
One of the most distinctive aspects of kathakali makeup is the chutti – a white "frame" that focuses the audience's attention on the actor's face. Traditionally, the makeup artist constructs the chutti from specially cut paper and inserts it into layers of rice paste. Applying the chutti takes at least an hour.

*Dancers dust their faces with yellow powder*

*A special seed, the chundapoo, is washed, cut, and inserted into the eyelid to make the eyes look bloodshot*

**BEAUTY CONTESTS FOR MEN**
The Woodabe people of Niger, West Africa, hold dancing competitions so the women can decide which man is the most attractive. A contestant uses makeup to emphasize his eyes, his long, thin nose, and his white teeth, and he uses facial expressions to show off his inner beauty.

**DRESSING ROOM**
Backstage at the ballet, dancers make themselves up in dressing rooms assigned according to rank: the more important the dancer, the bigger the dressing room. The corps de ballet share a space, but principal dancers have their own rooms and often their own makeup artists.

**3 MAKING THE EYES RED**
When the chutti is dry, the actor applies the rest of his makeup. As a final touch, he cuts a seed known as a chundapoo and inserts it into his eyelid. The cut seed dyes the white of the eye red, and this highlights the expressive eye movements that are a major part of a kathakali performance.

The heavy kiritam
(headdress) is made
of wood and inlaid
with imitation
gemstones

## SPECTACLE OF KATHAKALI
Kathakali narrates the heroic adventures from India's two
most famous epics, the *Mahabharata* and the *Ramayana*.
Dealing with the constant struggle between good and evil,
kathakali is highly spectacular and often involves a fierce
battle that results in the destruction of a supernatural
demon. The ornaments, movements, and especially the
costumes and makeup emphasize the sacred nature of
the characters. Noble-hearted heroes always have
green faces, while actors playing treacherous
schemers paint their faces dark red or black.

Coconut shell,
holding rice paste

Erkila

Spirit
gum

Chutti coil

Paper to
make chutti

Paints

## COLORS AND TOOLS
Rocks are ground up and
mixed with coconut oil to
produce the vivid paints
used by kathakali actors.
Spirit gum and then rice
paste are applied with a
chutti coil to paste the chutti
paper to the actor's face.

The kiritam is
usually painted
in red, green,
white, and gold

The eyebrows
and eyes are
exaggerated with
black makeup

## ABORIGINAL DREAMING
In central Australia,
Aboriginal dancers apply
ocher and soft feathers to
their bodies in geometrical
designs. The designs and
makeup have great religious
importance, linking the
dancers to their ancestor
spirits and to the Dreamtime
– the time of Creation.

# Costumes in dance

Dance costumes enhance a performance in a wide variety of ways. For example, in traditions where there are no stage sets, costumes help the audience make sense of the action. Costumes often follow specific codes; for example, the size of a headdress or the length of a sleeve may say something about the character. Costumes can be stunning in themselves, but their impact is usually reinforced with makeup, music, and gesture. This combination immediately helps an audience tell the loyal from the treacherous, the good from the wicked, and the admirable from the despicable. Costumes can veil, obstruct, round out, or emphasize the contour of the dancers' bodies and movements. They add a whole new dimension to dance.

*Warriors often wear long pheasant feathers in their headdress*

*Graceful movements of the pheasant feathers are part of the dancer's gestures*

Nō kimono, Japan

*Opaque tights highlight the beautiful line of the leg*

**CHINESE OPERA**
In Chinese opera, warriors are important characters. They bring visual excitement with their acrobatic moves. Both male (wusheng) and female (wudan) warriors wear costumes that allow for ease of movement. Trousers enable the dancers to perform spectacular high kicks.

*Modern transparent material*

**ALL-IN-ONE COSTUMES**
Choreographers of western contemporary dance, such as Maurice Béjart of France, focus on the expressive power of movement. The all-in-one costume used in his work *Malraux* (1986) allows the spectators to see all the movements of the choreography.

**HISTORICAL COSTUME**
Costumes can indicate historical periods without being exact historical replicas. In Yolande Snaith's *Gorgeous Creatures*, the main character is recognizably Queen Elizabeth I of England. While her clothing is inspired by the period, it is made of modern material that allows for interesting dance movements.

### NŌ DRAMA, JAPAN
The kimono (left), worn in nō, transforms the proportions of the performer's body. The wide sleeves create a contrast between the overall pyramid shape and the narrowness of the wrists. In performance, a belt is placed well above the waist.

### PAVLOVA'S DYING SWAN
Michel Fokine's *La mort du cygne* (1905) became associated with Anna Pavlova just as, generations before, the name of Marie Taglioni conjured up a vision of *La Sylphide*. It is rumored that Pavlova's last words were about the dance and that she died clutching her costume (right).

*Real swan feathers made the costume realistic*

*Colorful, hand-embroidered motifs*

### GEORGIAN BALLET
Dancers of the Republic of Georgia wear very long costumes that hide their feet. When they move they seem to glide across the floor as if mounted on wheels, and the audience cannot see how the effect is achieved.

*Light, flowing material*

*Headdress size and design is determined by role*

*Red jacket symbolizes a heroic role, while demons wear black and Lord Krishna wears dark blue*

*Skirt is supported by many layers of cotton underskirts*

### KATHAKALI COSTUME
Kathakali performers wear extremely ornate clothing. The color of the jacket depends on the character; the jacket is open at the back so that the performer can be cooled by fanning. The vast skirt is made up of many layers of white cotton, with a decorated top layer. The performer varies the skirt's length by splaying his knees and legs.

*Outside of the foot bears the weight*

Masquerade costume, Nigeria

### IBO MASQUERADE COSTUME
Masquerade costumes hide the identity of the performer. Often padding is sewn in to exaggerate or create additional body parts. This costume is worn by the Ibo men of Nigeria, West Africa, who imitate young girls as part of the annual harvest celebrations. Traditionally, a mask completes the masquerade outfit.

# Costume design

*Vividly colored stripes resemble sunrise*

*Wide-sleeved coat*

**C**OSTUMES ARE AN IMPORTANT part of dance. In some traditions they act as a moving set – against a bare backdrop, they help place the characters in context. Costumes may complement or enlarge the movements of the dancers. In Chinese classical dance, performers wear long sleeves, which they manipulate to create beautiful shapes, while in Javanese classical dance and Spanish flamenco, female dancers kick back their trains. Some costumes have ancient origins: in India, the costumes of modern classical dancers are based on temple sculptures. Since costumes are a traditional element of most dances, they are not often redesigned for particular performances. However, they are usually adapted to make the most of modern technology: it is more convenient to use Velcro than hooks as fasteners. In western theater dance, however, innovation is highly valued as part of the dance experience, and dance costumes are regularly redesigned.

**CHINESE CONJUROR**
The Chinese conjuror (sorcerer) is one of the characters in *Parade* (1917), a ballet that satirizes a troupe of entertainers. Picasso's sketches for the magician's costume are outlandish, matching the tone of the ballet.

**PICASSO'S DESIGNS**
Pablo Picasso (1881–1973), one of the greatest artists of the 20th century, designed costumes for the ballet. From 1917, he worked with the Ballets Russes in Paris. Many of his first costumes for the ballet *Parade* were influenced by cubism, a style of modern art that Picasso founded. The costumes created a small sensation.

*Early costume designs for a prima ballerina*

*Rich but somber colors hint at melancholy theme of ballet*

*Sample costume fabrics*

**1 DESIGNING FOR THE BALLET**
At the start of the design process, the artistic director briefs the costume designer on the production. For example, the ballet might have a melancholy atmosphere in Act III, and the costumes need to reflect this. The designer then sketches early ideas. With some ballets, certain traditions must be observed: in a classical ballet, such as *Sleeping Beauty*, lead ballerinas always wear short costumes known as tutus. With newer ballets, designers can be more flexible.

*Paper patterns for costume*

**2 MAKING THE COSTUME**
The designer sketches ideas for every costume that will appear in the ballet. Once the director approves these ideas, the designer turns them into patterns – guides for cutting the fabric, usually made of paper or cardboard. The costume is then sewn, with alterations being made after it has been fitted to the dancer.

*Headdress of twisted gold echoes details of lace on cloak*

*Motif of vine leaves and grapes*

*Synthetic pearls form clusters of grapes*

**ALL IN THE DETAIL**
In major ballet productions, even the costumes for lesser characters are designed with great detail. The Cavalier of the Golden Vine is a minor character in the ballet *Sleeping Beauty.* Nonetheless, this costume from a 1946 production is lovingly embroidered, even though it would be almost impossible to see the details from the auditorium!

*Cloak is removed and hung up to become part of the set*

**4 USES FOR COSTUME**
When Eurydice first appears to Orpheus, she is weighed down with a heavy cloak. Since it is obviously uncomfortable for a dancer to perform in a heavy costume, the costume is designed so that the ballerina can remove the cloak after the initial impact of its appearance.

**3 INTO THE UNDERWORLD**
When Adonais Ballet Company decided to put on the new ballet *Orpheus,* costumes were commissioned that would reflect the story. The ballet is based on the Greek myth of the musician Orpheus, who is overcome with grief when his new wife Eurydice is killed, and descends to the dark shadows of the underworld to find her. Eurydice's costume is designed to show that she is now a spirit, trapped in this gloomy realm.

**5 PERFORMANCE**
The dancer now performs in a leotard and chiffon wrap. The wispy drapes still suggest the spirit world, but do not weigh the dancer down. The costume shows off her technique; here, the chiffon highlights the beautiful shape of the arabesque.

# Behind a mask

A DANCER'S FACE is one of the most expressive parts of the body, yet there are dances all over the world in which performers prefer to use masks to cover their faces. By concealing themselves behind masks, performers can let go of their own identities and devote themselves completely to the movements. Wearing masks challenges dancers to use their bodies in particular ways, so that every part becomes more expressive. In addition, masks can have a symbolic meaning: they may represent spirits or gods, dead ancestors, or the prized skills of a highly respected animal. Wearing a mask allows a performer to take on the special qualities of someone – or something – else.

**LITTLE OLD MEN DANCE MASKS, MEXICO**
Clownlike figures are part of many mask traditions. In the Mexican state of Michoacán, wooden masks painted pink represent the *viejito*, or little old man, a grandfather cavorting around in a humorous manner.

**WAR DANCE, PAPUA NEW GUINEA**
Men performing a war dance wear frightening masks, carry weapons, and cover their bodies with mud. Their dance represents the eternal battle between good and evil, light and darkness.

*Carved skulls add to the drama of the dance*

*Mask is lavishly gilded with gold leaf*

*Papier-mâché is molded and then painted*

**TIBETAN MOUNTAIN DANCERS**
In the Himalaya Mountains, dancers wear wooden masks painted in bright colors (left). The performers, moving in slow rhythm in time to deep-sounding drums, dance both on festive occasions and at times of ill fortune. Masks like this represent the spirits of their mountain gods.

*Boldly colored geometric designs*

**IBAN DAYAK, SARAWAK, BORNEO**
The Iban Dayak, Sarawak's largest native group, traditionally use painted wooden masks (left) at harvest festivals, when dancers celebrate the end of the harvest and the fertility of the land. These dances also celebrate the connection between Iban Dayak society and the cycle of the natural world.

**FÊTE DE MASQUES, IVORY COAST**
West African countries are famous for their mask dances. Masks are usually worn to conceal the identity of the performer. The Ivory Coast has a festival of masks every year.

**Bar supplies leverage to pull open the beak**

**Mask has a dual purpose: to represent the eagle and to reveal the human**

**RANGDA MASK, BALI, INDONESIA**
According to Hindu tradition, wives were killed when their husbands died. In Balinese dance, the unpopular rangda, or widow figure, represents women that survived. The witchlike rangda possesses dangerous magical powers – only the strongest performer can withstand her spirit.

*Rangda is depicted as shaggy and wild*

*Drawstring pulls the mask aside to reveal the human face beneath*

*Rangda has fangs and a long, hanging tongue to devour children*

**KWAKIUTL**
Among the Kwakiutl of the American Northwest, traditional priest-doctors called shamans often wear masks during ceremonies. These connect the shamans with the powers of their ancestors. The masks often represent admired creatures, such as the eagle depicted here.

**COURT DANCE, THAILAND**
In Thai court dances, beautifully ornate papier-mâché masks, featuring an elaborate golden top, are worn by male dancers to celebrate special occasions such as the king's birthday. Although Thailand is a Buddhist country, court dances usually depict one of the great Hindu epics. One such story, the *Ramayana*, relates the heroic deeds of the god Vishnu in his disguise as Rama, the king of Ayodhya.

*Realistic costumes and masks*

**ANIMAL MASKS**
For a ballet based on the tales of Beatrix Potter, costumes and masks – neatly arranged in the Royal Ballet's storeroom when not in use – re-created each animal character in minute detail. Although the masks and costumes were inhibiting, the dancers transmitted the personality of each character – such as the delightful Squirrel Nutkin, pictured above – through their movements, which were brilliantly choreographed by the British dancer and choreographer Frederick Ashton (1904–1988).

# Dance and worship

*Expressive eyes and hands are most important*

**AN ANCIENT ART**
In India, practically all performing arts have close links with religion. Bharata natya is linked to ancient temple dances in Tamil Nadu, southern India. The dancers came from special families and were known as devadasis.

DANCE BRINGS TOGETHER thoughts and feelings, and can create special, deeply felt emotions. In some areas of the world, such as Australia, India, Africa, and parts of western Asia, certain dances are linked to religion and are regarded as sacred: to those dancers, dancing is a form of prayer. Even in places where dance is not connected with worship, dancers say that the experience can be transcendental – in other words, it is a way to leave everyday life behind and climb into the realm of the spirit.

*This dance movement closely resembles one of the popular postures of Siva, the Indian lord of the dance*

**DEVADASIS IN THE COMMUNITY**
In traditional Indian society, secular and religious activities were not clearly separated. Devadasis and their dances were important for rituals such as weddings, as well as for entertainment in royal courts.

*Pleats are practical as well as beautiful*

**WHIRLING DERVISHES**
The dervishes are Muslim friars, originally from Turkey. When dancing, they spin around faster and faster with their arms spread out until eventually they enter a trancelike state. In this higher state of mind, they believe it is possible to be in contact with God.

Necklace

Anklet

Hair ornament

*Anklets add percussion to the moves*

**DANCING TO REACH THE DREAMTIME**
In Australia, Aboriginal people dance as a way of reaching a timeless zone they call the Dreamtime. According to ancient belief, this was when the universe and everything in it was created. Dancing the sacred dances re-creates the universe and helps keep everything in its proper order.

**COSTUME AND JEWELRY**
When bharata natya was reconstructed in the 1930s, the costume was based on temple sculptures and everyday life. Most Hindu statues are adorned with jewelry, so this became part of the look. Since devadasis used to be dedicated to the temple god by being symbolically married to him, the costume has become popular with brides.

*Ornaments and jewelry resemble those of a bride in Tamil Nadu, India*

## MOVING THROUGH SPACE
When performing in a confined space, bharata natya dancers suggest space through the use of their body and particularly their eyes, rather than through large movements across a floor.

*Ogun, the god of iron, blacksmiths, and war*

## BHARATA NATYA TODAY
Today, bharata natya is performed in theaters as a solo concert dance. The modern art form combines elements of mood, music, and drama. The term comes from joining together parts of the words *Bhava* (emotion), *Raga* (melody), *Tala* (rhythm), and *Natya* (drama). The expressiveness of the dancer, rather than her pure athletic ability, is bharata natya's most important quality. Although dancers are no longer married to the gods, bharata natya is often based on stories of gods, goddesses, and heavenly nymphs, and a performance always begins and ends with a dedication to God.

## DANCE STAFF, NIGERIA
The Yoruba of Nigeria use iron dance staffs to mark the distinctive rhythms for dances associated with individual gods. Each staff is connected to a particular god.

*Jewelry and flowers make the dancer resemble Hindu statues*

*Circle of fire*

*Hand shapes and movements are precise*

Medieval bronze of Siva Nataraja

*A demon crushed by Siva*

## LORD OF THE DANCE
Siva Nataraja, the Indian lord of the dance, is just one aspect of the great Hindu god Siva. The four-armed Siva Nataraja is always shown dancing. He represents the creation-death-regeneration cycle of the universe.

## RUTH ST. DENIS
Ruth St. Denis (1877–1968), one of the pioneers of American modern dance, sought to celebrate the spiritual in her dances. She looked for inspiration in mythologies from around the world, and she created many exotic dances based on her idea of what she called "the Orient." Though these dances were immensely popular, they were far from authentic.

*Pleats fan out to reinforce the shape of the dance*

# Court dance and pageantry

SPECIAL DANCES, known as court dances, have been used throughout history to represent the ruling powers. All over the world, these ruling powers have also made sumptuous and spectacular pageants a part of court life. These great spectacles displayed both their wealth and their control over vast numbers of people. Special court dances – regal and measured in their movements and performed on significant national occasions, for example – reinforced the sense that a king is somehow different from his people and strengthened the position of a ruler. Court dances tend to be different from other dances. They are hierarchical, setting those at the source of power apart from the ordinary folk. Court dances have had far-reaching effects – they have given rise to the classical forms of dance in Europe, Asia, and Africa.

*Bugaku performers were traditionally male but were made up to perform female roles*

*Kimonos used for bugaku are splendidly decorated*

*Mask represents Matsubara, a dragon king*

*Mask is made of wood, lacquer, and human hair*

**BUGAKU COURT DANCE**
The bugaku and gagaku of Japan represent the world's oldest unbroken tradition of court dance and music. Some of today's performers claim they are 39th generation – that members of their family have performed these dances and music throughout the last 1,200 years! Some dances depict legendary battles, while others tell the story of meetings with supernatural beings and mythical beasts. The costume for bugaku often includes spectacular face masks.

*Long, full kimonos are used for the more serious bugaku, which are known as "left" dances*

**A NATIONAL TREASURE**
Bugaku is a dance of great dignity and stateliness in which the performers move very slowly and elegantly in simple symmetrical patterns. For centuries, only the imperial household, government officials, and their guests were allowed to enjoy bugaku – the public could watch only after World War II. Today, these court dances are seen as reflecting qualities in the Japanese national character, and in 1995, bugaku and gagaku performers were proclaimed "living national treasures."

**OCTOBER 1 PARADE, BEIJING, CHINA**
In China, one of the major celebrations is the National Day festival on October 1, which commemorates the day in 1949 that the Communist Party swept to power after years of revolution and established the People's Republic of China. A love of pageantry and display comes to the fore at festivals such as this, with colorful and perfectly synchronized fan dances such as the one performed above.

*The striking of stately poses is central to bugaku*

**COURT DANCE, GHANA**
Carried by his courtiers, the elected king of the Ashanti in Ghana makes an impressive entrance. On special occasions, the king dances before his people to display his royal virtues. His dance movements are powerful but slow and dignified. The royal umbrella shading the king is also made to "dance" in time to the drums.

Ashanti finger rings, made of gold and encrusted with jewels

Golden Ashanti daggers

**SUN EMBLEM**
History remembers Louis XIV of France as *le roi soleil* – the Sun King. In 1653, at age 15, Louis performed as the rising sun in *Le ballet de la nuit*. In 1654, he performed as Apollo, the Greek sun god, in *Les noces de Pelée et de Thétis*. His costumes were liberally decorated with images of the sun.

**ASHANTI GOLD**
Arab travelers in the 8th century described Ghana as "the land of gold," and for centuries gold has been the Ashanti people's emblem. Even today the king may dance while weighed down with masses of gold jewelry and ornaments. In the past, the golden heads of heroic Ashanti kings decorated the royal throne, and a gold stool symbolized the unity of the nation.

*Costume features emblems representing the sun*

**DANCE AT THE COURT OF LOUIS XIV**
During his reign, Louis XIV drew the aristocracy to Versailles, his court outside Paris. The king was a well-known lover of dance; to be invited to dance in his presence was an honor that could launch a career, and Louis himself often performed. There was, however, an ulterior motive to Louis' court dances. By forcing the aristocrats to spend lavishly to keep up with his extravagance while also keeping them away from their bases of power in the provinces, Louis kept them under his control financially and politically.

**EUROPEAN COURT DANCE**
In the 16th century, European princes competed with each other to have the most sumptuous court, emptying their treasuries to stage extravagant spectacles. In 1581, Catherine de' Medici and her son Henri III organized a royal wedding that included a series of court balls. These balls, held at the Louvre in Paris, were so lavish that they set the standard for all subsequent celebrations.

Louis XIV as the rising sun, *Le ballet de la nuit*, 1653

# National heritage

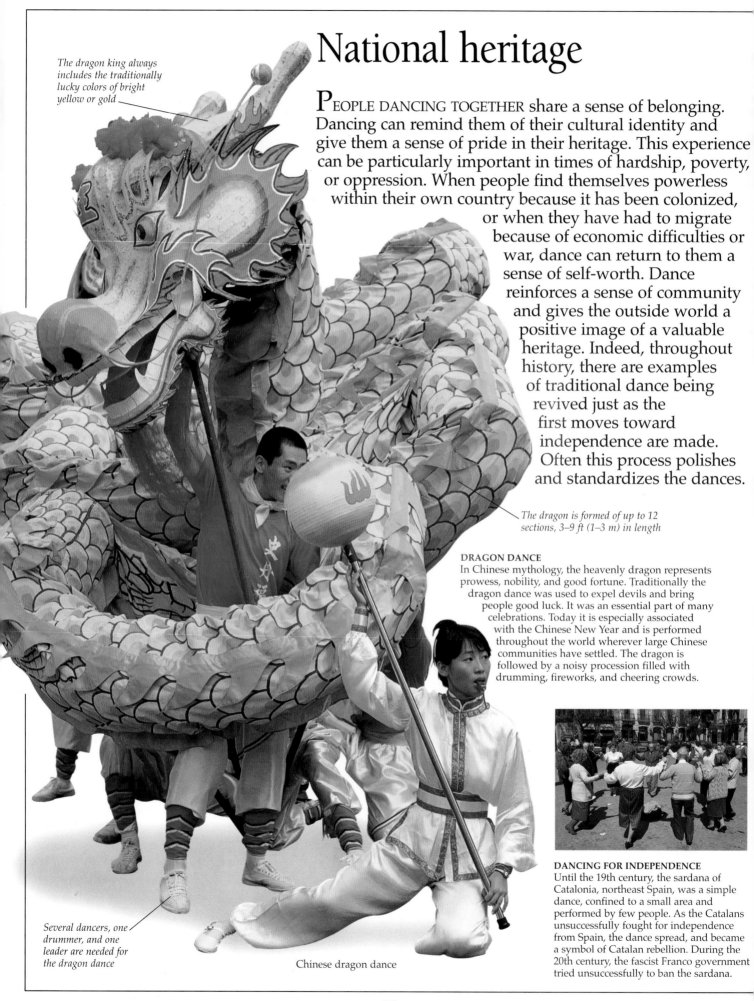

*The dragon king always includes the traditionally lucky colors of bright yellow or gold*

Pᴇᴏᴘʟᴇ ᴅᴀɴᴄɪɴɢ ᴛᴏɢᴇᴛʜᴇʀ share a sense of belonging. Dancing can remind them of their cultural identity and give them a sense of pride in their heritage. This experience can be particularly important in times of hardship, poverty, or oppression. When people find themselves powerless within their own country because it has been colonized, or when they have had to migrate because of economic difficulties or war, dance can return to them a sense of self-worth. Dance reinforces a sense of community and gives the outside world a positive image of a valuable heritage. Indeed, throughout history, there are examples of traditional dance being revived just as the first moves toward independence are made. Often this process polishes and standardizes the dances.

*The dragon is formed of up to 12 sections, 3–9 ft (1–3 m) in length*

### DRAGON DANCE
In Chinese mythology, the heavenly dragon represents prowess, nobility, and good fortune. Traditionally the dragon dance was used to expel devils and bring people good luck. It was an essential part of many celebrations. Today it is especially associated with the Chinese New Year and is performed throughout the world wherever large Chinese communities have settled. The dragon is followed by a noisy procession filled with drumming, fireworks, and cheering crowds.

### DANCING FOR INDEPENDENCE
Until the 19th century, the sardana of Catalonia, northeast Spain, was a simple dance, confined to a small area and performed by few people. As the Catalans unsuccessfully fought for independence from Spain, the dance spread, and became a symbol of Catalan rebellion. During the 20th century, the fascist Franco government tried unsuccessfully to ban the sardana.

*Several dancers, one drummer, and one leader are needed for the dragon dance*

Chinese dragon dance

### QUETZAL DANCE, MEXICO
In an effort to rediscover their preconquest identity, native Mexicans organized themselves into dance associations. At festivals and all-night vigils they perform traditional Aztec dances – some of which are named after Aztec gods, including the most powerful god of all, Quetzalcoatl.

*Pheasant feathers*

Quetzalcoatl, the fabulous Aztec plumed serpent god of light

Headdress

Back of an Irish dance costume

*Irish symbol of the shamrock*

*Green, white, and gold were favorite colors*

*Irish rose of handmade lace*

### ORISSI, EASTERN INDIA
The classical Indian dance orissi was at one time performed only by temple dancers called mahari. Like other classical forms, it was the subject of a cultural revival from 1930 to 1950, just as serious moves toward independence from Great Britain were being made.

Orissi dancer

Ute chief in tribal dress

### IRISH DANCE AND IDENTITY
At the turn of the century, traditional Irish dance changed from an informal pastime into a symbol of nationalism. Dances were standardized, and costumes became highly decorative. They were often adorned with Celtic designs copied from a 9th-century illuminated manuscript, the *Book of Kells*, which had just been discovered. Irish dance helped create an image of Irish nationhood.

Soft dance shoes

Kikuyu dancers performing a courtship dance

### NATIVE AMERICAN POWWOW
White Americans frowned upon large intertribal gatherings, or powwows, because they felt threatened. In the 1930s, as Native Americans feared the loss of their cultural identity, they turned powwows into dance competitions, in which the dances of a glorious native past could be passed down to younger generations.

*Soft shoes allowed for intricate movements in dances, such as the slip jig*

### KIKUYU DANCERS, KENYA
In many East African societies young couples traditionally perform courtship dances. These dancers are performing such a dance for tourists, using adapted traditional movements.

# Role reversal

WOMEN MAY DANCE AS MEN, and men as women, for a number of reasons. For example, in France in the late 19th century, ballet dancing had become a female activity, and women took over the male roles. The male lead in *Coppelia* (1870) was choreographed for a ballerina called Eugénie Fiocre. In 17th- and 18th-century China and Japan, it was considered improper for women to go on stage, so some male performers began to specialize in female roles. Role reversal is often thought of as humorous. All over the world, there are pantomimes featuring men dressed as women – the humor lies in the fact that the performers are obviously male and wear outrageous costumes. On the other hand, the Venda people of South Africa use role reversal in dance for a serious reason – it helps confuse evil spirits who might otherwise harm the dancers. Today in dance, the more common role reversal involves a male dancer playing a female role.

**GROTESQUE FEMALE ROLES**
In romantic ballet, female dancers represent the essence of beauty and elegance. There is a convention in ballet that such beauty cannot perform ugly roles, so these roles are performed by men dressed as women. In Frederick Ashton's *La fille mal gardée* (1960), Lise, the daughter of Widow Simone, loves Colas, but her mother is determined to marry her to Alain, the feeble-minded heir of a rich farmer. The ballet is full of slapstick and comic effects, both in the characters and in the choreography.

**SALOME BY BÉJART**
Only 10 lines are devoted to Salome in the Bible, yet her story has been portrayed and elaborated in all the arts, especially dance. Invited to dance at court in celebration of Herod's birthday, Salome pleased the king so much that she was allowed to ask for whatever she wanted. Her mother advised her to demand John the Baptist's head. Salome has usually been portrayed as a sensual woman, but the French choreographer Maurice Béjart wanted to break the stereotype of the female seductress and cast a man in the role.

*Widow Simone, a caricature of a woman played by a man, here resembles a pantomime dame*

## CARABOSSE IN *SLEEPING BEAUTY*

The evil fairy Carabosse in *Sleeping Beauty* (1890), the Ugly Sisters in *Cinderella* (1948), and Widow Simone in *La fille mal gardée* (1960) are all comic or grotesque female roles played by men. In *Sleeping Beauty*, Carabosse places a curse on a baby princess. The curse is meant to kill her, but a good fairy, Lilac, changes it so that it makes the princess and her family sleep for 100 years.

Carabosse (right) in *Sleeping Beauty*

False hips

Crinoline

## CARABOSSE'S COSTUME

The role of the reclusive Carabosse is traditionally danced by a man. As the evil fairy moves menacingly around the stage, her earthy, wicked nature is often depicted by a costume that enlarges her body with false hips and a crinoline. Over these Carabosse wears a dress of dusty, ragged black.

## SWAN LAKE, ADVENTURES IN MOTION PICTURES

Matthew Bourne's version of *Swan Lake*, choreographed in 1995, stunned audiences. The ballet features no dainty ballerinas. Instead, the swans are bare-chested men in feathery pantaloons, who convey both birdlike grace and a ferocity unknown in more traditional versions. They represent the assertive and masculine side of the male lead, Prince Siegfried, instead of the feminine grace and elegance of the lead ballerina, Odette/Odile.

## KABUKI ONNAGATA

In many Japanese classical dance forms, only men were allowed to perform publicly. Since plays contained female roles as well as male, some actors specialized in these. In the traditional dance form known as kabuki, these specialists are called onnagata, which means woman-person. Elaborate makeup and costume help transform a mature man into a beautiful young woman, but the main transformation takes place in the gestures, bearing, and voice of the performer. Kabuki actors are trained not only to move like women on stage but also to think like women.

*An onnagata headdress is often extremely ornate*

*Costumes can weigh up to 40 lb (18 kg) and are lavishly decorated*

*Kabuki kimonos are designed so they can be removed to transform the dancer into another character*

# Something old, something new

From the time they were rediscovered, the painted and carved images of ancient Greek dancers have inspired modern dancers, including Isadora Duncan, who have admired and emulated their elegance.

DANCE LINKS PAST and present, ancient and modern. For dance to be properly appreciated, it needs to create images that are understood by its audience: if a dance is too remote, people will not be able to make sense of it. Dancers use the traditions of the past in various ways and for a number of reasons. Some reject tradition because they feel it is not relevant to the present – they want to create dances that address contemporary issues. Others feel that they want to rediscover a golden, more meaningful past. Yet others see their work as the logical development of a thriving tradition.

**LOOKING FOR INSPIRATION**
The American dancer Isadora Duncan (1878–1927) is the figure most noted for loosening the restrictions of ballet, which she considered unnatural and damaging. In her search for the real source of dance, she turned first to the art of classical Greece, second to nature, and third to herself. She once claimed her style of dance was "the art lost for two thousand years."

*Duncan's clothing and costume were also inspired by ancient Greece*

*Motifs found on Greek friezes adorned the fabric of Duncan's costumes*

*Wildflowers are often embroidered in bright colors on folk costumes for both men and women*

**COPPELIA**
In the ballet *Coppelia* (1870), a young man named Franz becomes so smitten with the charm of a mysterious "girl" that he forgets his fiancée, Swanilda. The girl, however, is nothing but a doll. The dancers' costumes are inspired by a romantic idea of what central European peasantry might once have worn. Swanilda wears a blouse with puffed sleeves and an embroidered bodice over a wide skirt.

*Garland of flowers on Swanilda's romantic tutu indicates that she is a village girl*

**FOLK DANCE IN BALLET**
Many ballets incorporate elements of folk dance. In the first act of *Coppelia*, for example, the dancers perform a stylized version of the Polish dance mazurka. Traces of other European dances, such as the Italian tarantella and the Hungarian czardas, have found their way into the ballet. This type of dancing is known as character dancing.

## BUTOH EXPERIMENTAL DANCE, JAPAN

Butoh is Japan's best-known postwar experimental dance. With butoh, dancer and choreographer Tatsumi Hijikata (1928–1986) and his colleagues aimed to startle the Japanese into recognizing some of the unpleasant aspects of their society. They called their style of dancing ankoku butoh – the "dance of the dark soul." Even though butoh was a conscious attempt to break away from tradition, some elements remain rooted in classical dance. One of these elements is the very slow, stylized walk sometimes used in butoh, which can also be seen in nō.

*Masklike makeup resembles the controlled faces of the dance form kabuki*

*Shaved heads represent a rejection of the wigs of traditional dance*

*Trash cans and lids provide percussion*

## STOMPING FORWARD IN TAP

In Britain in the late 1980s, some young dancers got together and founded a company called Tap Dogs. Rather than use conventional musical instruments as accompaniment, they explored the use of everyday and incongruous objects. The result was *Stomp*, an energetic and exhilarating work performed with great gusto.

*Young men in magnificent costumes display fast and difficult footwork in the "fancy dance" contest of the powwow*

*Austere costumes are far removed from the elaborate kimonos of kabuki, nō, and bugaku*

## A COMMON HERITAGE

Among Native Americans, two types of dance traditions coexist. One is performed within individual tribal groups and fosters that group's identity. The other is performed by many tribal groups and fosters an overall Native American identity. Contemporary powwows (singing and dancing gatherings) feature a "fancy dance" contest.

# Changes over time

THERE IS NO SINGLE HISTORY of dance; there are, rather, many histories of many dances around the world. However, all dances are rooted in the past, because they either embrace the traditions of the past, or try to break away from them. We know of some dance traditions, such as those of ancient Greece, because the Greeks left clues in their paintings and sculptures. We know of other histories, such as how classical ballet developed, because teachers have left behind notes on steps or style. We can trace the history of western theater dance back about 350 years, but other traditions, such as some of Japan's classical dance forms, go back some 1,200 years. But even these dances are not unchanged relics – performers are always progressing and always innovating.

**MARIE TAGLIONI**
When the Italian star dancer Marie Taglioni (1804–1884) performed *La Sylphide* in 1832, she wore calf-length flowing costumes and pointe shoes to give the audience a full view of her flawless technique. Her success created such a demand for dancing on pointe that classical ballet was changed forever.

Shoes from *The Rite of Spring*

**RITE OF SPRING**
*The Rite of Spring,* a ballet about an adolescent girl dancing herself to death as a sacrifice to the god of spring, was first performed in Paris in 1913 and immediately caused a scandal. Igor Stravinsky's discordant music and Vaslav Nijinsky's ground-breaking choreography shocked an audience fed on conventional grace and beauty.

*Stiff bodice was difficult to move in*

A 17th-century ballet costume

*Longer skirt than modern costumes*

*Costumes were sumptuous with gold and silver thread on silk*

*Female dancers are the stars of Fokine's* Les Sylphides

**LES SYLPHIDES**
The popular one-act ballet *Les Sylphides* has only the barest of story lines: A poet is dazed by the presence of beautiful sylphs. With this work, first performed in 1909, the Russian choreographer Michel Fokine proved that ballet could survive and do well without being based on a complex dramatic situation.

**COSTUME CHANGE**
In 1760, the French choreographer Jean-Georges Noverre (1727–1810) wrote his *Lettres sur la danse et sur les ballets* (*Letters on Dancing*) as a reaction against the conventions that fettered French ballet. He appealed to dancers to take off their "enormous wigs and gigantic headdresses which destroy the true proportion of the head with the body" and to discard the "stiff and cumbersome hoops which detract from the beauties of execution."

**RUSSIAN BALLET**

ROYAL OPERA
COVENT GARDEN
· SEASON 1912 ·

SIXPENCE NET          LONDON · JOHN LONG Lᵀᴰ

**DIAGHILEV'S BALLETS RUSSES**
Sergei Diaghilev's ballet company brought together the talents of the most modern dancers, designers, composers, and choreographers. From 1909 to 1929, it toured Europe and the U.S., and established ballet as a major theater art.

*Shorter tutu allowed classical ballerinas to show off their form and technique*

A modern tutu

*Rhinestone decoration glistens in the stage lights*

**MARIE CAMARGO**
When the Belgian dancer Marie Camargo (1710–1770) first shortened her skirt to her ankles in 1726 to show off her entrechats (jumps in which the feet cross in the air before landing), she shocked traditionalists. Men's dance costume had always been designed to allow for leaps and spins, but it was not until the 19th century that all women dancers finally began wearing a lighter, less cumbersome costume – a tutu – that allowed greater freedom of movement.

**MODERN BALLET AND DANCE**
By the early 20th century, ballet was seen as restrictive and rigid, so choreographers simplified costumes and invented new movements. In 1992, American dancer and choreographer Twyla Tharp restaged *Push Comes to Shove* (1976) for the Royal Ballet, with moves that were very different from the classical style.

*An off-balance movement in Push Comes to Shove*

*Modern ballet footwork can look angular compared with classical ballet*

*Curved arms, held en haut, or high up*

*Feet point outward with heels together*

First position

*Feet are spaced*

*Erect torso with the spine acting as the center*

Second position

Third position

*Legs turned out from the hips, so body is open toward the front*

Fourth position

Fifth position

**CENTURIES OF TRADITION AND TECHNIQUE**
All dance traditions are grounded in technique. Dancers go through a progression of movements and exercises that create the ideal physique for each style. Ballet, for example, is based on five classical positions devised by Pierre Beauchamp (c.1631–1705) around 1700. The five positions lay down basic rules for ballet.

# Groups and shapes

SOMETIMES THE RELATIONSHIP between dancers produces patterns that create specific dance formations. Group dances can be divided into two types. In the first, dancers keep their places within the formation throughout the dance: whether the dancers move in a circle, in straight lines, in figure eights, or in spirals, they remain in line and are led by the dance leader. In the second type, dancers change places through movements including chains, crossings, bridges, or stars. They dance independently within a dance, but interact with other dancers at different times. Each dancer usually ends up back in his or her starting position.

## KOREAN FAN DANCERS
Dancers can carry props to create beautiful and colorful shapes in the air. For example, some traditional Korean dancers use large fans to extend their movements. Grouped together, the shapes and movements of the fan dancers create a stunning spectacle.

## SQUARE DANCING
Modern square dancing is largely derived from a 19th-century European dance known as the quadrille, where four couples danced in a square formation. In the modern square dance, couples may change partners, or exchange places, or take turns dancing alone. The figures can be quite complex, and a caller shouts out instructions.

*In many dances, male dancers hold each other's hands or a handkerchief*

*The dance leader often performs his own improvised steps*

*The traditional skirt is known as a foustanella*

## GREEK DANCING
Many dances in Greece are performed in open circles: the dancers form a chain, holding each other by the hands, waists, or shoulders and move in a circle. The first and last positions are clearly distinguished. The leader can take the chain wherever he or she wants. The order taken by the dancers usually reflects seniority. Commonly, men are at the beginning of a chain in descending order of age, followed by women, also ranked according to age.

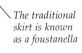

*In Hindu mythology, the gods create the universe by dancing in a magnificent circular formation, kicking away the dust of chaos as they go*

## IN THE ROUND
The circle is a very common dance formation. It can move either clockwise or counterclockwise. Any central figures in a circle may have special significance. Most often the dancers in a circle are on equal terms with one another – everyone can see everyone else – and they usually have to move in unison.

*Krishna is often represented as a heavenly dancer*

## FORMATIONS IN MUSICALS
American musicals developed the Eastern European folk tradition of the double story, in which dancers of one circle stand or sit on the shoulders of another circle. The musicals of the 1920s and 1930s achieved stunning visual effects based on the multiple story.

*Flower detail on muslin cloth echoes the pattern of the dance*

## MAYPOLES AROUND THE WORLD
The center of a circle is the focus of a circular dance. Maypole dances, in which participants dance around a long pole, exist everywhere. The pole often symbolizes fertility.

Bolivian tape dance

*Ribbons held by the dancer are twisted attractively one over another in the course of the dance*

An 18th-century embroidered muslin cloth showing Krishna dancing with the gopis (cowherds), North India

# Dance and community

WHETHER WE ARE watching or participating, dance is a way of uniting communities and is commonly linked to leisure, sport, and competition. Ballroom dancing is now one of the most popular recreations in the U.S. and Europe. Its beauty and romance allow both the dancers and the audience to escape reality. Meanwhile, in dance halls throughout the world, young people meet and let off steam on the dance floor. Carnivals – including the spectacular annual events of Rio de Janeiro and New Orleans – provide ample opportunity for entertainment and merrymaking, and in many areas folk dances preserve the traditions of the past while giving a sense of well-being to the participants.

*Female dancers wear exquisite gowns, often embroidered with rhinestones*

*Partners make imperceptible signals with their index fingers to indicate changes in rhythm or steps*

*For some dances, such as the waltz, male dancers dress formally in white tie and tails*

*Feathers enhance the dancer's graceful movements*

**BALLROOM DANCING**
At hundreds of clubs in Great Britain and Europe, thousands of people attend ballroom-dancing classes in order to learn the skills necessary to attend tea dances and enter competitions. Ballroom dancing was popularized by Irene and Vernon Castle in the US in the 1910s. Today, fans of the waltz, fox trot, cha-cha, and quickstep feel that this sophisticated style of dancing, with its melodic accompaniment and beautiful costumes, is reminiscent of an earlier, more elegant time.

## ORIGINS OF BALLROOM DANCE
Contemporary ballroom dancing grew out of several traditions. Regional dances performed by the common people were the basis for many of these dances. In the 16th century, traveling dance masters began teaching both "city" and "country" styles of dance, and the two styles influenced each other. By the 19th century, aristocratic gatherings such as the ball depicted above, also contributed to the tradition. By the 20th century this style of dance was further enriched by the inclusion of African influences.

## CARNIVAL
Both in Europe and in the Americas, carnivals have allowed people to dance in the streets and generally turn the social order upside down. For this reason, the authorities have often frowned upon carnival merrymaking

## FOLK DANCE
The Industrial Revolution in Europe inspired nostalgia for an idealized golden past – a time when peasants enjoyed traditional country pursuits. This interest in the life of the common country people widened to include dance, and in 1893 a Folk Dance Society was set up in Stockholm, Sweden. Many more such societies followed in other parts of Europe in an attempt to rescue vanishing folk cultures.

Swedish folk dancers in traditional dress

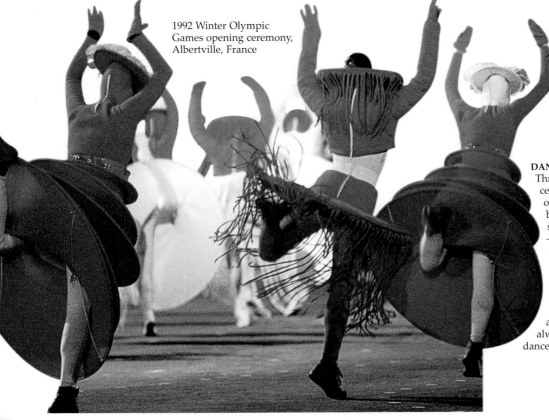

1992 Winter Olympic Games opening ceremony, Albertville, France

*Bold movements and vivid costumes could be seen from a distance*

## DANCE AND CEREMONY
Throughout history, as rituals and ceremonies became meaningless or were lost, they were replaced by new ones. In modern times, sport is one of the last remaining – and most important – pursuits that people enjoy together. Pageantry and ritual surround major sporting events. The Winter Olympic Games are watched by people all over the world. The spectacular opening and closing ceremonies are always marked by presentational dance and pageant.

Paris dance hall, late 19th century

## EARLY DANCE HALLS
Ordinary people were generally excluded from the elegant balls held by the aristocracy. By the late 18th century, they began to establish public dance halls of their own for the enjoyment of dancing. By the 1890s, people in large cities were flocking to halls, such as the one shown here to dance and have a good time.

# Sets for dance

DANCE CAN BE PERFORMED in all sorts of surroundings, from the most elaborate theater stage to a clearing in the bush. The place where the dance is performed is known as the set. A set has a great influence on the relationship between dancers and audience. Its appearance is dictated by the location and the type of dance – for example, a processional street dance must have a mobile set, if it has one at all. Western theaters tend to have more lavish sets, while Asian theaters (with the exception of the complex sets often used for Japanese kabuki) tend to have fixed, plain backgrounds. If there is no set, performers must bring a story to life by means of their bodies alone, making the audience "see" the voyages, hunts, or battles taking place.

**DANCING IN THE STREET**
Street parades, such as this festival in Japan, invite a community to take over public spaces and celebrate in dance. Open-air dance is more appropriate to audience participation than theater performances.

**SET DESIGN FOR** *SWAN LAKE,* **1989**
Set is all-important in establishing the mood of a ballet. This model is for the ballroom in Act III of *Swan Lake,* one of the most famous and popular classical ballets of all time. With its score by the 19th-century Russian composer Peter Ilyich Tchaikovsky, the set was designed to evoke a regal atmosphere by placing *Swan Lake* in the court of the Russian czar. The set features fantasy elements combined with accurate historical details. The jewels, heavy loops of gold, and imperial purple drapes all convey the magnificence of the czar's palaces.

Original sketch for the 1943 set

**UPDATING SET DESIGNS FOR** *SWAN LAKE,* **1943**
The British Royal Ballet performed *Swan Lake* to audiences of thousands against a set that was first designed in 1943. The old set and costumes were updated in 1989, giving a different look to one of the world's favorite ballets and creating a different atmosphere for new generations of ballet-goers. The production, costumes, and sets were all transformed by designer Yolande Sonnabend.

Set model for production of *Swan Lake* at the Royal Opera House, London, 1989

## SWAN LAKE, ACT III

The ballroom scene, shown here, is at the center of *Swan Lake*. During the ball, Prince Siegfried is deceived into proposing marriage to Odile, the daughter of the evil sorcerer, Rothbart. Rothbart watches gleefully as the pair dance a glorious pas de deux.

*The queen's throne*

*Lady-in-waiting*

*The evil sorceror Rothbart*

*Prince Siegfried's mother, the queen*

## GOING TO A DISCO

Discotheques – nightclubs where people dance primarily to recorded music (rather than live) – were introduced in the 1950s but were most popular in the late 1970s and 1980s. Large clubs were filled with crowds, and featured lasers and light shows to create a fantastic environment. Record companies helped discos become more popular by releasing disco singles and generating big money for the entertainment industry.

*Ornamental details evoke a sense of fantasy*

*Bejeweled set inspired by the Russian court jeweler, Fabergé*

*Queen's throne*

*Sketch looks menacing*

*Puttin' on the Ritz, set design, 1929*

*Movements make the actual set less menacing*

*Puttin' on the Ritz, actual set, 1929*

## DANCE SETS AND HOLLYWOOD

Some of the most amazing dance sets ever seen were created for Hollywood musicals such as *Puttin' on the Ritz* by Busby Berkeley (1895–1976). Having introduced sound to the movies in 1927, producers fed the cinema-going public song-and-dance extravaganzas as a vehicle for the new technology. The spectacular sets successfully held the audience's attention despite sometimes weak plots and scripts! Berkeley was a master at lavish musicals – even today, the dance settings in his movies seem fantastically imaginative.

# Behind the scenes

WHEN WE THINK ABOUT theater dance we think first of dancers, then of choreographers, then – possibly – of composers, musicians, and designers. Many more people, however, are involved behind the scenes in dance productions. Dance is full of nondancers: notators who write down steps and restage works; lighting designers who transform moods and enrich the sets; teachers and therapists who keep dancers' bodies finely tuned; people who look after shoes, costumes, and wigs; sound technicians, stagehands, painters, carpenters, box office personnel, front office managers, public relations people, administrators, critics . . . the list is endless! Most of these people never make a dance movement or are even seen by an audience. Nonetheless, they are an integral part of dance, and no performance can take place without their input. Dance productions are a cooperative venture, both on and off the stage.

### SHOE MISTRESS OR MASTER
Dancers often wear special shoes, such as pointe shoes, which are specifically designed for their type of dancing. A shoe mistress or master needs to look after the shoes, making sure that they are in good condition, that they are the right color for the costumes, and that they are replaced when necessary.

*Scale model for* The Nutcracker

### STAGE SETS
To create the set – the scenery on the stage – the designer discusses the overall vision with the choreographer before designing the set on paper. When these ideas are approved, an accurate scale model is usually built to see if the design works in three dimensions. When built, the design may be altered until the artistic director feels it is just right.

Paints and paintbrush

*Lighting rig*

### LIGHTING
Stage lights can create a huge variety of moods and impressions, and enhance the theater sets and dance costumes. In the ballet *Petrushka*, for example, blue lights are used to give the cold feeling of a Russian winter. Lights hung above the stage and in the auditorium are referred to as the rig. The rig is controlled electronically from a central box.

Painting the set for *Alice in Wonderland*, 1995

*Massive flowers give a fanciful, fairy-tale impression*

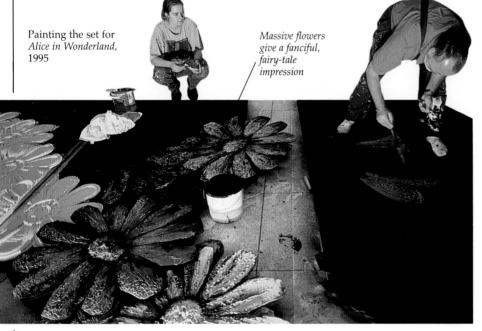

### PAINTERS AND CARPENTERS
Once the sets are designed, they have to be made to create the impression presented on paper. Background scenes may be painted onto backdrops. Alternatively, they may be built out of wood, with windows and doors through which dancers can enter and leave the stage. The sets need to be maintained as they are moved in and out of the theater and taken on tour.

## WARMING UP

Prior to a performance, dancers need to warm up onstage at a portable barre brought in by stagehands. They may start with pliés or knee bends, or they may have their own exercise routines. The warm-up gradually builds up include strenuous exercises involving the feet, ankles, and knees. Good warm-up is crucial to dancers to prevent them from injuring their muscles. Dancers wear a variety of casual, comfortable clothing to keep them warm before getting into their costumes.

*Small scissors are used to cut thread*

*Pins are used to hold fabric together before sewing*

A pair of small needlework scissors and pins

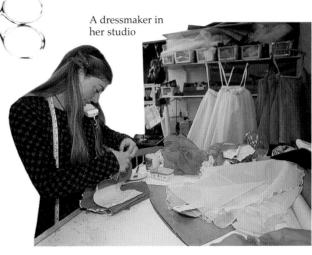
A dressmaker in her studio

## MAKING COSTUMES

Costume designers make detailed sketches of their ideas and often attach samples of possible fabrics. These are given to skilled dressmakers and tailors who then turn the designs into costumes. Costumes must never restrict movements. Sleeves must allow the arms to move freely, and fastenings must be comfortable for the dancer, but also allow for quick changes. Costumiers, as they are sometimes called, can become close to the dancers they dress. Anna Pavlova's personal dresser, Manya Charchevenikova, stayed with the great dancer until her death, becoming an intimate and privileged friend.

Makeup brushes and lipstick

## MAKING UP

Makeup is used to accentuate a dancer's features. It must be quite vivid and applied heavily so that dancers' faces can be seen under strong stage lighting. Different makeup can create different expressions, such as mournfulness or fierceness. Sometimes it can completely change the shape of a dancer's face, especially if "putty" is used to make a false nose or chin. Makeup for beautiful characters, such as the Sugar Plum Fairy in *The Nutcracker*, concentrates on eyes and lips.

Warming up at a portable barre

*Specially lit mirror is needed to ensure that makeup can be seen under lights*

Making up for *The Nutcracker*

# Famous dancers

**RUKMINI DEVI**
Inspired by Anna Pavlova, Rukmini Devi (1904–1986) dedicated her life to the revival of classical dance in her native India, enchanting audiences by her performances.

A DANCE EXISTS ONLY while it is being performed – and yet sometimes a performance can leave an impression so strong that it stays in the memory forever. Some dancers dazzle audiences with their technical skills and physical prowess, while others stir us emotionally, through their special ability to interpret a story. Few dancers are capable of both in equal measure, but those who are often become so famous that their names go down in history. In fact, dance history is largely the history of the most famous dancers – unique performers and teachers who devoted their lives to dance, such as Anna Pavlova, Vaslav Nijinsky, and Rukmini Devi. In the eyes of the world, their names are legendary and have come to symbolize the dance they loved so much.

*Pavlova's main talent lay in her expressive movements*

**KATHERINE DUNHAM**
An exceptionally skilled and admired dancer, choreographer, and scholar, Katherine Dunham (born 1910) created a completely original dance technique in the late 1930s. She combined ballet with movements from African and Caribbean dance traditions.
Dunham is often seen as a major figure in African-American dance, but in fact her pioneering technique is very much part of mainstream modern dance.

Pavlova as a bacchante (a dancing girl from Greek mythology)

Dunham founded her own dance school in 1945

Rogers and Astaire in *Roberta* (1935)

**ANNA PAVLOVA**
To the thousands who saw her perform – and the millions who know her name – the Russian ballerina Anna Pavlova (1881–1931) was the essence of ballet. An outstandingly expressive performer, she was famous for her ability to interpret a story. Pavlova once said that she wanted to "dance for everybody in the world," and she toured constantly. From 1910 to 1925, she visited Europe, the Americas, Asia, and South Africa, performing nearly 4,000 times and inspiring many dancers and choreographers.

**FRED ASTAIRE AND GINGER ROGERS**
A film producer once told dancer Fred Astaire (1899–1987) that he could only "dance a little." Astaire, with dance partner Ginger Rogers (1911–1995), later became an international star. Gracefully anticipating each other's smallest movements, the pair expressed perfectly the romance of ballroom dancing.

Nijinsky in his costume as a faun, for the ballet *L'Après-midi d'un faune*

*Nijinsky's mystical costume was created by Russian designer Léon Bakst*

Martha Graham in *Salem Shore* (1941)

## MARTHA GRAHAM

To most people, breathing is a mundane fact of life. To dancer Martha Graham (1894–1991), it was a fascinating process. From her observations of breathing, she developed the principles of "contraction and release," on which she based her pioneering style of modern dance.

## JORGE DONN

Born in Argentina, ballet dancer Jorge Donn (1947–1992) was famous for his powers of interpretation. His flawless technique enabled him to use his whole body to communicate with an audience.

## VASLAV NIJINSKY

Russian dance legend Vaslav Nijinsky (1890–1950) is best remembered for his remarkable jumps, or elevations. In the 1911 ballet *Le Spectre de la Rose*, in which he portrayed the spirit of a rose, he soared out of a window into the night, creating probably the most famous leap in ballet history. Nijinsky was also famous for his controversial choreographies, such as *L'Après-midi d'un faune* (1912). On its opening night, members of the audience alleged that this ballet was obscene, and fights broke out.

# Choreography

THE WORD *CHOREOGRAPHY* comes from the Greek *graphia*, meaning "to write down," and *choros*, meaning "dance." Today, choreography refers more to the invention of dances than to the mere writing down of dance steps, and a choreographer is an inventor of a new sequence of dance steps. The importance of the choreographer varies from one society to another. In Japan, some classical dances have been choreographed and are performed only by specific families. In many African and European folk dances, some dance steps are remembered and handed down through generations – they may be named after their choreographers. In Western theater dance like ballet, choreography is a profession and choreographers can become world-famous.

Perrot with Carlotta Grisi, for whom he choreographed *Giselle* (1841)

**JULES PERROT**
During his lifetime, Jules Perrot (1810–1894) created expressive choreography that helped tell the story of his ballets through movement. His convincing characters came from all social classes, but his heroes were frequently of humble origins.

**MARIE RAMBERT**
Trained in a method of rhythmic analysis known as eurythmics, Polish-born Marie Rambert (1888–1982) studied in Paris. While there, she was hired by Sergei Diaghilev of the Ballets Russes to help dancers with the complex score of *The Rite of Spring*. In 1931, she established Britain's first permanent ballet company and school in London, and nurtured the talents of famous choreographers, including Frederick Ashton.

*Lean, long-legged dancers were ideal for Balanchine's type of work*

**GEORGE BALANCHINE**
The name of George Balanchine (1904–1983) is synonymous with American classical ballet. Originally from Russia, Balanchine emigrated to the U.S. and set up the School of American Ballet in 1934, planting the seed for the future New York City Ballet (1948). Balanchine's swift, athletic style came to be seen as distinctively American.

Balanchine (center) demonstrating a pas de deux position, 1950

## MERCE CUNNINGHAM
After working with Martha Graham, the American dancer Merce Cunningham (born 1919) developed his own original style. Although he worked out his dance movements in some detail, their order was left up to the performers – or even determined by flipping a coin! In his choreographies, he gives equal importance to each area of the stage and sees sound, decor, and movement as independent entities.

The position of this dancer is recorded in Benesh movement notation (BMN), below right

*In BMN, five horizontal lines represent the level of the head, shoulders, waist, knees, and floor*

*Hands are held above the head*

*Elbows and knees are indicated by crossing basic signs*

| | | Head |
| --- | --- | --- |
| | | Shoulder |
| | | Waist |
| | | Knees |

*Floor*

## BENESH MOVEMENT NOTATION
Benesh movement notation, or BMN, was developed in England in the 1940s by Rudolf and Joan Benesh. It is a movement – rather than dance – notation, and can record what the body does in any activity, whether it is ballet or football. Today many dance companies employ Benesh notators to write down scores of the choreographies in their repertoire.

*des Vaisseaux*  41

*Musical score is included to ensure that music and steps complement each other*

*Step symbols are placed beside a central line*

*Right and left are shown by placement of symbols on either side of the central line*

Feuillet's notation system

## NOTATION SYSTEM
In 1701, a French dancing master, Raoul Feuillet (c.1675–c.1730), wrote his *Chorégraphie ou l'art d'écrire la danse (Choreography or the Art of Writing Dance),* giving a notation system for writing down basic movements, rather than the conventional steps that everyone knew. The system quickly became accepted by dance masters throughout Europe. It allowed them to recreate each other's choreographies with a minimum of effort.

*Central line shows the floor pattern of the dance*

*Left hand is in front of the body with palm facing front*

*Right foot is raised to waist level behind the body*

*Right arm is raised to shoulder level behind the body*

Position of body in BMN as seen from the dancer's point of view

*Left foot is on pointe*

## ARABESQUE IN BMN
This arabesque is notated as a static picture. A full score would indicate how the dancer moves into and out of the position as well as her timing. The left arm is raised in front of the body (vertical dash) above the head, the right arm is behind (a dot) at shoulder level. The left foot is on pointe, level with the body (horizontal dash), while the right foot is raised behind the body.

57

# Dance crazes

Dancing is a part of every society's culture – and a dance craze can test a society's tolerance levels. The history of dance in Europe and the U.S. shows how some dances that today represent elegance and sophistication were once thought deeply shocking. For example, polite society was appalled when the waltz was introduced because for the first time men and women danced in a close embrace instead of at arm's length. Some dances were deemed so outrageous that they were outlawed. In the 1910s, one woman spent 50 days in jail for dancing a banned dance called the turkey trot! Despite such reactions, fashionable people through the ages have wanted to learn the latest crazes.

**SHOCKING WALTZ**
In the 1780s, the waltz gripped Germany. At first people frowned upon the abandonment of the whirling couples and claimed that the dance was weakening the bodies and minds of the younger generation.

**DOING THE CAKEWALK**
The cakewalk was a craze of the 1890s. The dance originated on sugarcane plantations, where, after harvest, plantation owners would set up a dance competition for their enslaved African workers. The slaves who made up the fanciest dance steps won cakes. The cakewalk, with its strutlike steps, broke the tradition of smooth, gliding dances that had been dominant in the past.

*A strutting style is characteristic of cakewalking*

**CHARLESTON**
In the 1920s, the charleston conquered New York. Its origins dated back to World War I, when many African-Americans left the poverty of the southern states to work in New York's munitions factories. They brought with them a high-stepping dance style, which was featured in popular African-American musicals, such as *Runnin' Wild*. From the shows, the craze spread all over the city and to all sections of society.

*Sometimes dancers knocked hats off the heads of their audience with their spectacular high kicks*

*Cancan dancers lifted and swirled the fronts of their dresses*

*The cancan's finale eventually featured splits*

*Toulouse-Lautrec's "Moulin Rouge"*

**CANCAN AT THE MOULIN ROUGE**
In the 1830s, the cancan, featuring a line of high-kicking women, hit Parisian ballrooms. As the cancan became more wild and acrobatic, it was seen by many as immoral. By the 1880s, the cancan had moved into music halls, such as the Moulin Rouge. The French artist Henri de Toulouse-Lautrec (1864–1901) immortalized the dance in his posters.

### ROCK 'N' ROLL DANCERS

In the 1950s, rock 'n' roll music and dance were all the rage. Couples moved exuberantly around the dance floor, reinventing old steps from the charleston and the lindy hop (a fast, improvised 1930s dance). Partners showed off to friends with acrobatic moves such as "air steps," in which the man spun his partner through the air.

*In rock 'n' roll dancing, the man leads his partner through different moves*

*Chubby Checker, who had a hit single called "The Twist"*

### LET'S TWIST AGAIN

The twist caught on in the 1960s. It brought a development as revolutionary as the first closed-couple waltz – partners let go of each other! They stepped apart to wriggle and shake on their own. No one led, no one followed, no one even needed to know the steps!

*The leading dancer always holds his partner's right hand with his own left hand*

*Light-up heels*

*Adapter for recharging batteries in shoes*

*Dancers try to make even difficult moves look effortless*

### DISCO MANIA

Dancers have always invented dramatic outfits: red boots for tango, beaded fringed dresses for the charleston – even sandals with flashing lights for disco. These "disco shoes," complete with batteries, became fashionable after the movie *Saturday Night Fever* was released in 1977, and disco became the hottest dance craze of its time.

# Did you know?

## FASCINATING FACTS

Rock art found in southern Africa shows prehistoric dancers. The paintings were made by the San people over a period of about 10,000 years. San shamans took part in trancelike dances performed to harness the energies of the spirit world.

Prehistoric rock art of San dancers

The leotard is named after its inventor, Jules Léotard, a French acrobat who performed the first flying trapeze act on November 12, 1859. He wore a tight-fitting outfit to show off his muscles.

Dance star Joaquín Cortés was born in Cordoba, Spain, in 1969 and joined the Spanish National Ballet at 15. In 1992, he formed the Joaquín Cortés Flamenco Ballet. His *Pasión Gitana* (*Gypsy Passion*) has been enjoyed by more than a million people around the world.

Spanish-born Joaquín Cortés in performance

The youngest ballerinas ever to play leading roles were the "Baby Ballerinas" who joined the Ballets Russes in 1933: Irina Baronova was just 13, Tamara Toumanova was 14, and Tatiana Riabouchinska was 15. The girls starred in ballets choreographed by the great George Balanchine.

Florenz Ziegfeld was the creator of the *Ziegfeld Follies*, a revue show that ran on Broadway from 1907 to 1931. The *Follies* featured comic sketches, songs, and dance routines from the longest-ever chorus line. A film based on the show, directed by Vincente Minnelli, came out in 1946.

Each spring, the Cherry Blossom Dance is performed by novice geishas in the Japanese city of Kyoto. The girls dance on a stage strewn with pink-and-white cherry blossoms to the accompaniment of traditional instruments, such as the banjolike shamisen.

The Dance of the Seven Veils is based on the journey of a Mesopotamian goddess to the underworld. At each of the seven gates, Ishtar had to "take off" one of her powers; in the dance, the performer sheds the seven veils that cover her body.

In ancient Greek mythology, the nine muses were patron goddesses, each associated with one of the arts. Terpsichore was the muse associated with dancing.

Nureyev plays Romeo to Fonteyn's Juliet

The most curtain calls for a ballet was 89, after Rudolf Nureyev and Margot Fonteyn danced in *Swan Lake* in Vienna, Austria, in 1964. The duo also delighted audiences in *Romeo and Juliet*, *Giselle*, *Marguerite and Armand*, and *Les Sylphides*.

Some pop songs have their own dance. Michael Jackson created the "moonwalk" for his hit *Thriller* in 1982, while Madonna caused a stir with the "vogue" in 1990.

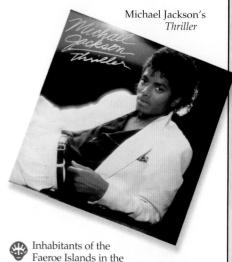

Michael Jackson's *Thriller*

Inhabitants of the Faeroe Islands in the Atlantic Ocean perform circle dances. The Faeroese are descendants of Norwegian Vikings. They dance in time to sung ballads that tell of young heroes who defeat trolls, dwarfs, and giants.

The most popular ballet is Tchaikovsky's *The Nutcracker*, which was first performed in 1892. The ballet, based on a fantastical tale by German writer Ernst Hoffmann, includes the famous Dance of the Sugar Plum Fairy. Tchaikovsky wrote the music to two other great ballets: *Swan Lake* and *The Sleeping Beauty*.

An old engraving of a Lipizzaner and rider

## Q Which horses are trained to dance?

A Lipizzaner stallions dance at the Spanish Riding School in Vienna, Austria. The finale of a Lipizzaner display is often the Grand Quadrille, a dance that involves up to eight horses (and riders), all in step. Lipizzaners were also used in 2002 by the American choreographer Paula Josa-Jones. Her piece *Ride* featured six horses and riders, along with seven modern dancers.

Line dancers

## Q What is the most popular dance in the world today?

A Improvised moves are more popular than any set steps. However, around the world there are thousands of clubs and millions of dancers devoted to line dancing, a type of folk dance where the dancers are always in rows and move from back to front in a square formation.

A perfomance of *Riverdance*

## Q Who turned Carmen into a car mechanic?

A Carmen is the passionate gypsy heroine from the opera *Carmen*, written by 19th-century French composer Georges Bizet and first performed in Paris, France, in 1875. In the dramatic finale, Carmen is killed by a jealous lover. British choreographer and director Matthew Bourne created a new ballet, *The Car Man* (2000), based on the opera. Famous for his gender-bending *Swan Lake* (see p. 41), Bourne cast a male dancer in the Carmen role. Luca is a handsome drifter who takes a job as a car mechanic at Dino's Garage. However, just like Carmen, Luca's magnetic good looks soon provoke jealousy – and dark tragedy.

## Q Which is the longest-running musical?

A Andrew Lloyd Webber's *Cats* closed on Broadway in 2000 after nearly 18 years of sellout performances. The musical was also the longest-running in London's West End. *Cats* is based on *Old Possum's Book of Practical Cats*, a collection of poems by T.S. Eliot. Feline characters, including Old Deuteronomy, Grizabella, and Mister Mistoffelees, all performed their own songs and dances.

## Q Who was the world's most highly paid dancer?

A Michael Flatley entered the record books in 1999 as the world's highest-paid dancer, earning $1.8 million a week. His legs were insured for $44.7 million. Chicago-born Flatley made his name in 1994 with *Riverdance*, an Irish dance routine for the Eurovision Song Contest. The following year, it was turned into a full-length show. His *Lord of the Dance* (1996) and *Feet of Flames* (1998) have also been enjoyed by millions worldwide.

Matthew Bourne's *The Car Man*, a modern reworking of *Carmen*

## Record Breakers

✺ **BIGGEST DANCE**
Around 72,000 people gathered to do the chicken dance at a fair in Ohio in 1996.

✺ **BIGGEST TAP DANCE**
The biggest tap dance involved 6,952 dancers and was held in Stuttgart, Germany, in 1998.

✺ **FASTEST TAP DANCER**
At his fastest, Irish dancer Michael Donnellan can make 40 taps a second!

✺ **MOST TURNS IN A BALLET**
Ballerina Pierina Legnani performed 32 *fouettés* (furiously fast turns on one foot) as Odile/Odette in *Swan Lake*. Ever since, everyone playing that role has had to try and do the same.

✺ **FARTHEST DANCE**
In 1996 David Meenan tap-danced a distance of more than 23 miles (37 km).

✺ **LONGEST CONGA**
Nearly 120,000 people joined in the conga in Miami, Florida, on March 13, 1988.

# World of dance

AMONG THE TRADITIONAL DANCES performed by people around the world are many different types of folk dances. Some date back thousands of years, while others have been created more recently, to express new experiences. Energetic or soulful, sacred or political, all these dances bring people together.

An Indian classical dancer

## AUSTRALIA & OCEANIA

Australian Aborigines and New Zealand Maoris have kept traditional dances alive. So have the peoples from other South Sea islands, such as Hawaii and Tahiti.

Hawaiian dancers

### HULA DANCING
*Hula kahiko,* or ancient hula, uses dance and chanting to retell Hawaii's history. The dance has its roots in ancient rituals performed by men to thank the gods. Today, *hula auwana,* or modern hula, is also performed – simply to express happiness.

## NORTH AMERICA

Native Americans have their own dances, such as the drum dances performed by Canadian Inuit. White settlers brought folk dances from Europe. In the 20th century, America led the way in popular dances, from jazz dancing to rock and roll and disco.

### STREET STYLE
In 1969, artist Afrika Bambaataa encouraged youths from poor areas of New York City to start the first breakdancing crews. With a portable stereo (boom box) playing hip-hop music as accompaniment, the kids danced acrobatically.

Breakdancing in New York City

## SOUTH & CENTRAL AMERICA

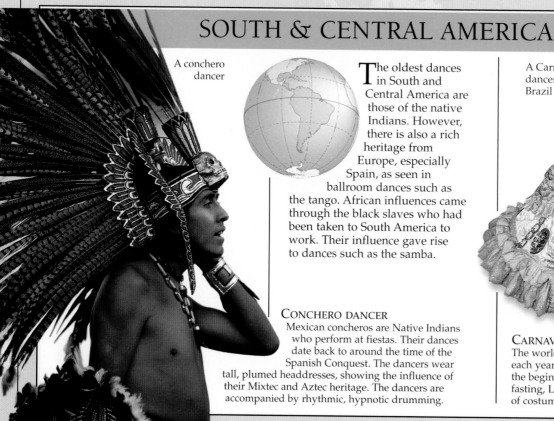

A conchero dancer

The oldest dances in South and Central America are those of the native Indians. However, there is also a rich heritage from Europe, especially Spain, as seen in ballroom dances such as the tango. African influences came through the black slaves who had been taken to South America to work. Their influence gave rise to dances such as the samba.

### CONCHERO DANCER
Mexican concheros are Native Indians who perform at fiestas. Their dances date back to around the time of the Spanish Conquest. The dancers wear tall, plumed headdresses, showing the influence of their Mixtec and Aztec heritage. The dancers are accompanied by rhythmic, hypnotic drumming.

A Carnaval dancer, Brazil

### CARNAVAL
The world's biggest dance festival is held each year in Rio de Janeiro, Brazil, to mark the beginning of the Christian period of fasting, Lent. For five days, "schools" of costumed dancers parade the streets.

# EUROPE

**D**ances of Europe include the waltz, polka, and flamenco. Many are couple dances, for a man and woman. Europe is also the birthplace of ballet, which originated in France in the 17th century.

### DANISH DANCE
Every year in Denmark, there are two big festivals of folk music and dance: one at Skagen in June and the other at Tønder in August. Dances include the fast-moving pols, which was popular in the 1600s.

Danish children folk dancing

### PORTUGUESE FADO
The fado is a multicultural undulating dance. The dance itself comes from the rhythmic traditions of Africans and Brazilians living in 19th-century Lisbon, Portugal. But the accompaniments are Portuguese guitar and traditional sung ballads.

*A fado dancer takes a rest*

From the painting *O Fado* (1910) by José Malhoa

# AFRICA

**A**frican dances are often performed for a function: to prepare for war, to give thanks, or to mark the stages in people's lives. In West Africa, dancers frequently wear sculpted masks.

Swazi men dance during the incwala

### INCWALA
Incwala is the name of a five-day harvest festival held in Swaziland, southern Africa. On the third day, the king performs a sacred dance to please his Swazi ancestors; then he eats the first pumpkin of the harvest. After the king tosses away the rind, his people sing and dance before feasting on the first fruits of the year.

# ASIA

### THAI DANCE
In Thailand, traditional temple dancers wear intricate gilded costumes. Their dance is a form of prayer and meditation. Every movement is elegant, precise, and controlled.

**A**sia is the world's largest continent. It is also home to a wide variety of dance traditions, such as the belly dances of the Middle East, the classical dances of India, and the elaborate, theatrical court dances of China, Japan, and Korea.

A Thai dancer kneels at Erawan Shrine, Bangkok

A Chinese dragon welcomes the New Year in Hong Kong

### CHINESE NEW YEAR
To celebrate the new year, Chinese people gather in the streets to watch dancing lions and dragons. Inside each costume, there may be 50 dancers or more. The dragon is associated with long life and prosperity.

# Find out more

Are you a dance fan? Here are some ways that you can find out more about dance. You will be able to see artists performing by visiting the theater or even by watching television – dance is an important part of many movies, especially romantic musicals. Many theaters also give behind-the-scenes tours, so that you can see sets close up. Visit your library for books about famous dancers or the history of dance. You can also study dance at many schools and colleges. Best of all, attend a dance class – whether you go for ballet, tap, or salsa, it is sure to be fun.

## USEFUL WEB SITES

- Wonderful online ballet dictionary by the American Ballet Theater
  **www.abt.org/education/dictionary/**
- The Texas Ballet Theater has a great kids' section on its Web site
  **www.texasballettheater.org/Kids/**
- Web site dedicated to Indian classical dance
  **www.tarang-classical-indian-music.com**
- Teen site covering all aspects of dance
  **www.young-dancers.org**
- Folk dancing Web site
  **www.folkdancing.org**

### DANCE THERAPY
Dance has the power to make people feel good. Therapists harness that power and use it to enrich the lives of people who are physically handicapped or trapped by mental illness. Performing expressive body movements can give people of all abilities a sense of great freedom and release.

*Julie Diana and Yuri Possokhov in The Sandpaper Ballet*

### BALLROOM DANCE ON THE BIG SCREEN
Movie-goers were introduced to the seductive world of Latin ballroom dancing with *Tango* (1998). The movie follows an Argentinian film director, Mario Suarez (played by Miguel Ángel Solá), who wants to make the best-ever tango film. In the process, Suarez falls in love with a beautiful, talented young dancer, Elena (played by Mía Maestro).

### NEW BALLETS
While many ballet performances are old classics, exciting new ballets are being written, too. *The Sandpaper Ballet* was first performed by the San Francisco Ballet in 1999. It was set to music by the American composer Leroy Anderson, and one of the pieces sounds just like someone scratching sandpaper.

## SYLVIE GUILLEM
Every generation of dancers has its stars, and it is well worth trying to see them perform. French prima ballerina Sylvie Guillem is one. In 2000 she danced as Marguerite in Frederick Ashton's *Marguerite and Armand*, a part originally written for Margot Fonteyn. Guillem was the first ballerina since Fonteyn whom the Ashton Estate has allowed to perform the dance.

*Together, the arms form an extended line.*

### PARIS OPERA OPULENCE
If you are lucky enough to be in Paris, France, visit the Opéra de Paris Garnier. The building itself, with its sculptures and friezes, is a work of art. However, to the dance enthusiast, it is most interesting as the home of the world's oldest ballet company, founded by Jean-Baptiste Lully in 1672. Nearby, the Musée de l'Opéra has a collection of memorabilia, including ballet slippers that belonged to Vaslav Nijinsky.

*Guillem dances en pointe*

### A GLIMPSE BACKSTAGE
Many theaters, including London's Royal Opera House above, allow visitors to visit behind the scenes when there are no performances. Tourists can see how the lighting rigs work and where the orchestra sits. They can also see where all the costumes are stored, and look at the dancers' dressing rooms.

# Places to visit

**SAN FRANCISCO BALLET, SAN FRANCISCO, CALIFORNIA**
www.sfballet.org
A world-class ballet troupe with performances of classics and new work. If you can't catch this troupe, check with theaters to see which companies are planning to appear in your area.

**CHILDREN'S MUSEUM OF DENVER, DENVER, COLORADO**
(303) 433-7444
www.cmdenver.org
A special section called Arts a la Carte is dedicated to the performing and visual arts. There's a dance floor, a puppet stage, and an artist's studio.

**METROPOLITAN MUSEUM OF ART, NEW YORK, NEW YORK**
www.met.org
(212) 535-7710
Includes masks, costumes, and instruments from Africa and the Americas, plus a unique costume collection with dance outfits and examples of traditional folk dress

**NATIONAL MUSEUM OF DANCE AND HALL OF FAME, SARATOGA SPRINGS, NEW YORK**
(518) 584-2225
www.dancemuseum.org
Features photographs, artifacts, and other exhibits showcasing all types of dance. Young visitors will enjoy the Discovery Room.

### THE HARD NUT
One of the most exciting things about going to see live performances is discovering how different choreographers interpret classic works – or even how stories can be adapted to different forms of dance. In Brussels, Belgium, in 1991, the Mark Morris Dance Group premiered *The Hard Nut* – an exciting new version of a favorite Tchaikovsky ballet, *The Nutcracker*.

# Glossary

**ACCOMPANIMENT** Music played to complement a dance and add drama

**ARABESQUE** In ballet, the movement where a dancer extends one leg back and one arm forward

**BALLET** A theatrical dance that tells a story to music.

**BALLROOM DANCING** Dancing in couples – either at social gatherings or in competitions. Dances performed include the fox-trot, waltz, cha-cha, and tango.

**BARRE** The handrail that dancers hold when they practice in a dance school

A can can dancer, painted by Henri de Toulouse-Lautrec

**BEDOYO** A Javanese court dance performed by women

**BHARATA NATYAM** A Hindu temple dance that originated in Madras, southeastern India. Dancers use hand gestures and facial expressions to interpret classical poems about the gods.

**BUFFALO DANCE** A ritual dance performed by Native Americans to give thanks to the gods for the buffalo

**BUGAKU** Japanese court dances accompanied by court music (gagaku), where dancers often wear elaborate masks

Dervish

**BUTOH** An experimental modern Japanese dance

**CAKEWALK** A ballroom dance dating from 1900, where dancers high-step and strut in a square formation

**CAN CAN** Performance dance popular in Paris in the 1800s. Lines of dancing girls lift their skirts to reveal multilayered petticoats as they high-kick to the music.

**CHA-CHA** A fast ballroom dance based on the Cuban mambo and popular in the 1950s. The steps are one, two, three, shuffle.

**CHARLESTON** Dance of the 1920s; involves steps and kicks to the front and back.

**CHINESE OPERA** Known in China as *ching-hsi*; a musical theater form, where the performers sing stories in Mandarin and make stylized movements

**CHOREOGRAPHER** Someone who invents sequences of dance moves, usually to music

**CONGA** An Afro-Cuban chain dance. The steps are one, two, three, kick.

**CORPS DE BALLET** The dancers in a ballet who perform together in a unified pattern, in contrast to the soloists

**COSSACK** A Russian soldier. Cossacks were famed for competitive, high-kicking dancing.

**CUECA** A Cuban folk dance performed by couples and accompanied by handclaps

**CZARDAS** Hungary's national dance, which starts slowly, then continues into a fast section where couples whirl and snap their heels

Flamenco dancer's costume

**DEMI-POINTE** In ballet, standing or dancing on the ball of the foot only

**DERVISH** A Sufi Muslim monk who whirls and chants in order to reach a trancelike state that brings him closer to God

**DEVADASI** An Indian temple dancer who performs the bharata natyam. The word means "handmaiden of god."

**DOMBA** A ritual chain dance practiced by young Venda women in South Africa

**DRAGON DANCE** Street dance performed by the Chinese, traditionally at New Year's, to frighten away evil spirits

**EN POINTE** In ballet, standing on the tip of the toes

**ENTRECHAT** A jump in which the dancer crosses the feet in the air

**FLAMENCO** A sensual Spanish gypsy dance performed to castanets and guitar music

**FOLK DANCE** Any traditional country dance

**FOX TROT** A ballroom dance popular in the 1910s

Square dancing

**GALLIARD** A lively European dance for couples, popular in the 1500s and 1600s

**GHOST DANCE** A dance performed by Native American Plains Indians to appeal to the gods to bring back the buffalo

**HAKA** A Maori war dance

**HIGHLAND DANCE** Energetic group dancing from the Scottish Highlands

**HULA** A sacred Hawaiian dance, where the women rock their hips back and forth

**IMPROVISATION** To spontaneously make up a dance, using no planned moves

Morris dancers

**IRISH DANCE** Folk dancing from Ireland, where the dancers hold their faces and torsos still, while moving their legs and feet quickly

**JAZZ DANCE** A rhythmic, improvized dance to jazz music

**KABUKI** A traditional Japanese dance-drama performed by men

**KATHAK** An energetic classical dance from northern India performed by both men and women, sometimes in pairs. The fast dances are interspersed with sections of mime.

**KATHAKALI** A classical dance-drama from Kerala, in southern India, which is usually performed by men and boys. Dancers mime to a sung story from a Hindu epic, such as the *Ramayana* or the *Mahabharata*.

A stage musical in Florida

Tap-shoe soles, showing metal "taps"

**LIMBO** A competitive West Indian dance. Dancers bend backward and shimmy under a low bar.

**LINDY HOP** A fast, improvised dance from the 1930s

**LINE DANCE** A country dance, where people in lines perform steps in unison, often shouted out by a caller

**MAZURKA** A Polish circle dance performed to bagpipe music, with lots of foot stamping and heel clicking

**MORRIS DANCE** A traditional English folk dance performed by groups

**MUSICAL** A popular western form of theater, incorporating songs and dance

**NOH** A Japanese form of dance-drama that is slow moving and very powerful

**ORISSI** An ancient Indian temple dance from Orissa, eastern India

**PAS DE DEUX** In ballet, a dance for two performers, generally a man and a woman

**PLIÉ** In ballet, bending the knees while keeping the body upright

**QUETZAL DANCE** An Aztec dance performed to honor the supreme god Quetzalcoatl

**RELEVÉ** In ballet, the term for moving the body upward (a strong rise)

**RHYTHM** A dancer's timing system, based on a pattern of movement or sound

**SAMBA** A fast-moving Brazilian dance

**SCORE** Document in which dance steps, or musical notes, are written down

**SQUARE DANCE** A folk dance for groups of four couples, with the movements sung out by a caller

**SYMPHONY** A piece of music, usually in several contrasting sections. A symphony is written for the whole orchestra – strings, woodwind, brass, and percussion.

**TANGO** A passionate ballroom dance from Argentina. Couples take long steps and make dramatic pauses.

**TAP DANCE** Dance performed in tap shoes, which have pieces of metal attached to the sole and heel

**TARANTELLA** A flirtatious Italian folk dance performed by couples

**TURKEY TROT** An American ballroom dance popular in the 1910s. Couples imitate a turkey's walk, bobbing up and down.

**TUTU** A frilled skirt worn by ballerinas. The Romantic tutu is calf-length, while the classical tutu reveals all of the dancer's legs.

**TWIST** A dance popular in the 1960s, performed alone by shaking and twisting the hips

**VARIATION** In ballet, a solo dance

**WALTZ** A whirling ballroom dance popular in the 1800s (its name comes from the German word meaning "to spin"). The basic pattern is step, slide, step

Performing the waltz

# 72-page Eyewitness Titles

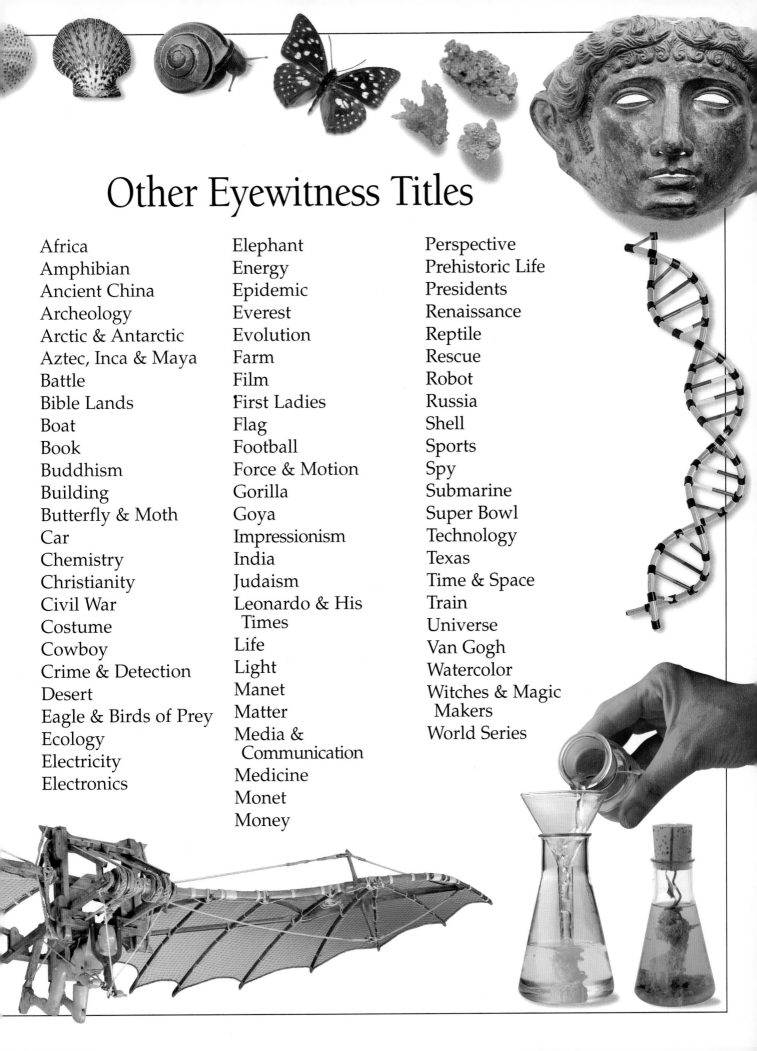

# Other Eyewitness Titles

# Index

# Acknowledgments

**The publisher would like to thank:**
Mary Shanley; Kalamandalam Vijayakumar at Kala Chethena Kathakali Troupe; Graham Mitchell and the Adonais Ballet Company; Indonesian Embassy and Gillian Roberts; Freed of London Ltd., for supply of ballet shoes; Anusha Subramanyam and Vipul Sangoi; Eric Pierrat at Gallimard Editions

**Editorial and research assistance:** Joanne Matthews, Katie Martin, Robert Graham
**Design assistance:** Goldy Broad, Maggie Tingle, Venice Shone, Elizabeth Nicola
**Additional photography:** Susanna Price, Gary Ombler

**Picture credits**
(t =top, b= bottom, c= center, l= left, r= right)
**AKG London:** 30tl (insert); Erich Lessing/Musee de Louvre, Paris 37bl. **Axiom:** Jim Holmes 10tl. **Patrick Baldwin:** 52tl, 52bl, 52cl, 53tr, 53bl, 53br. **Bata Shoe Museum, Canada:** 24tr, 25tc, 59cr. **Dominique Bernard:** 19tl. **Bibliothèque Nationale de France, Paris:** 29tr, 57cl. **Bridgeman Art Library:** Detail inside a Kylix from Vulci c.520–510BC British Museum, London 9br; Buffalo Dance by George Catlin (1794–1872) Location Unknown 18c; The Dancing Class, c.1873–76 by Edgar Degas (1834–1917) Musée d'Orsay, Paris, France 13tr; Pavlova as a Bacchante by Sir John Lavery (1856–1941) Glasgow Art Gallery and Museum 54tr; Poster for the Moulin Rouge, 1891 by Henri de Toulouse-Lautrec (1864–1901) Victoria & Albert Museum, London 58br. **Britstock-IFA:** F Aberham 36r. **Carroll & Brown:** 48c. **Christie's Images:** Angels & Bermans 30tl, Royal Opera House 31tr, A Ballroom Scene by Victor Gabriel Gilbert (1847–1935) 49tl. **Commonwealth Institute:** 29cl. **Dee Conway:** 9tr, 20bl, 21br, 28bc, 39tr, Kirov Ballet 20tr, The Georgian State Dance Company 29c, Adventures in Motion Pictures 41bl, Royal Festival Hall 43tr, Royal Ballet 33bc, 41bl, 45cr, Merce Cunningham Dance Company 57bl, 60bl, 60–61, 63bl. **Bill Cooper:** Birmingham Royal Ballet 17cl. **Corbis UK Ltd:** Bettmann/UPI 56bl; Bob Krist 68–9; Robbie Jack 44bl; John Marshall-Mantel 65tl. **Dominic Photography:** Catherine Ashmore 42br, 61tr, 65cr; Zoe Dominic 60tr. **Dover Publications, Inc.:** Great Ballet Prints of the Romantic Era, Parmenia Migel, 1981 44tl. **Enguerand-Iliade:** Agnès Courrault 41r; Colette Masson 28bl, 40tr, 43cl, 55cr. **Robert Estall Photo Agency:** Carol Beckwith 26bl. **E.T. Archive:** 51bl, 51cr; Royal Ballet Benevolent Fund 50bl; Victoria & Albert Museum 55l, Carlotta Grisi & Jules Perot in La Polka by J Bouvier, 1844 56tr. **Mary Evans Picture Library:** 8c(above), 12l, 37r, 42bl, 49br, 58cl, 58bl, 58tl. **Exeter City Museums and Art Gallery, Royal Albert Memorial Museum:** 4cl, 35cr. **Eye Ubiquitous:** David Cumming 19b; Matthew McKee 18br. **Gables:** 60tl. **Glasgow Museums:** St Mungo Museum of Religious Life and Art 35c. **The Granger Collection, New York:** 58tr. **Ronald Grant Archive:** 47tr. **Sally and Peter Greenhill:** 64tr. **The Horniman Museum London:** 4tl, 4bc, 6tl, 6tl(insert), 6cl, 9bc, 15tc, 15c, 15tcr, 15tr, 15cr, 15crr, 20tl, 32tr, 32c, 32bl, 33cr, 36c. **Hulton Getty:** 18bl, 35br, 55tr, 59l, 59tr. **Hutchison Library:** 8tr; Andre Singer 27br; Anna Tully 37tl; COJ Hatt 38br. **Image Bank:** A Boccaccio 49tc; David W Hamilton 39bl; Frans Lemmens 32br; Nicolas Russell 51tl; Steve Niedorf 52cr(below). **Images Colour Library:** 22cl, 26c. **Images of Africa Photobank:** David Keith Jones 25tr, 39bl. **Robbie Jack Photography:** 65tr, 65b. **Barnabas Kindersley:** 62br; photo from Children Just Like Me – Celebration! by Barnabas and Anabel Kindersley 67tl. **Kobal Collection:** MGM, 1952 8bl; RKO 54br; Tango © Argentine Sono 64C. **Vladimir Kozlick:** 64–65. **Macquitty International Photo Collection:** 14cl. **Musée d'Orsay** 66cl. **Novosti:** 23tr. **Panos Pictures:** Penny Tweedie 16tr. **Performing Arts Library:** 54tl, 54bl, 56cr; Ben Christopher 10bl; Clive Barda 26cl, 40bl; Emily Booth 17tl; Jane Mont 46tl; Marcelo Benoahan 12cr, 28br; Michael Diamond 45tl. **Pictor International:** 11bl, 11tl, 16bl, 38l, 43br, 46bl, 47br. **Rex Features:** 61cl, 61b, 62cl, 62cl, 63tl. **The Royal Ballet School:** 12 tr, 12 bl, 12 bc, 12 br, 13 bl, 13 cl, 13 cr, 13 br, 13 tc. **Sony UK Ltd:** 60cr. **Sotheby's Transparency Library:** The Dressing Room by Dame Laura Knight 1877–1970 © Dame Laura Knight, reproduced by permission of Curtis Brown Ltd, London 26bc. **South American Pictures:** Robert Francis 39tl; Sue Mann 14c; Tony Morrison Inc: Eric Brissaud / Gamma 36bl; Jo Pool / Gamma Press 49c. **Tony Stone Images:** Bruno de Hogues 14/15b; Chad Ehlers 49tr; Christopher Arnesen 32cl; David Hiser 32tl; Gerard Pile 34cl; Hugh Sitton 11r; Marcus Brooke 23cl; Penny Tweedie 34bl; Phil Schermeister 46cl; Rex A Butcher 50tl. **Angela Taylor:** Royal Ballet 51tr. **Telegraph Colour Library:** 17r. **V & A Picture Library:** 16br, 28tr, 44tr, 47c, 50/51b. **Wallace Collection:** 37cl(above), 37tl(below), 37l.

**Jacket images**
Front: Tl: © Archivo Iconografico, S.A./CORBIS; B: Anna Leon, 1999, Hilary Shedel/arenaPAL. Back: Carroll and Brown (c); Horniman Museum (cl, tc).